Growing Pains of the Soul

Growing Pains of the Soul

JOEL C. GREGORY

WORD BOOKS
PUBLISHER
WACO, TEXAS

A DIVISION OF
WORD, INCORPORATED

Library of Congress Cataloging-in-Publication Data

Gregory, Joel C., 1948–
    Growing pains of the soul.

    1. Christian life—Baptist authors. I. Title.
BV4501.2.G748 1987   248.4'861   87-23121
ISBN 0-8499-0626-1

Printed in the United States of America

898 RRD 98765432

And we pray this in order that you may live a life worthy of the Lord and may please him in every way: bearing fruit in every good work, growing in the knowledge of God, being strengthened with all power according to his glorious might so that you may have great endurance and patience. . . .

Colossians 1:10–11

Contents

Growing
Pains
of the Soul

Introduction

No pain, no gain." This is the contemporary motto of those who pump iron to build muscles. Yet what they admit in the physical realm we are reluctant to admit in the spiritual realm. Paul understood the truth of this spiritually: "For our light and momentary troubles are achieving for us an eternal glory that outweighs them all" (2 Cor. 4:17). Pressure and trouble are in the process of working out a future glory. No pain, no gain.

One man had the personal hobby of handcrafting violins. He focused on the kind of wood that made the best violin. He used all domestic woods. He imported foreign woods. He used aging processes to harden the woods. In all of it, the tone he desired from his violins rested beyond his reach. One day he found a gnarled piece of wood that came from the timberline. It had grown at that point where trees stop growing. The blasts of winter wind, the slashing rain, and the wind-swept bleakness of a mountaintop had twisted the wood and hardened it. Yet the violin created from wood taken at timberline produced a heavenly tone unlike anything else ever made. Timberline! It was a place of pain and of gain. God calls some of us to live at timberline where it is not easy, but that is where he puts the music in our lives. "I consider our present sufferings not worthy to be compared with the glory that will be revealed in us" (Rom. 8:18).

It is heat and pressure that make a diamond valuable. Ordinary coal in the bowels of the earth is placed under pressure of 1,500,000 pounds per square inch at a temperature of 5000 degrees F. Out of that heat and pressure the beauty of a diamond is born. We too have the raw materials within us to reflect the glory of God. Those raw materials can become radiant with splendor when we undergo the heat and pressure of growing pains.

A modern myth needs to be exploded. That myth maintains that great Christian character is forged without growing pains. That simply is not true. The great names of the Christian faith have all known incredible growing pains. John Wesley knew the pain of a terrible marriage. His wife even threw him around by the hair of his head! The first American missionary Adoniram Judson knew imprisonment in Burma, the loss of a child, and the death of two wives on the mission field. David Livingstone, the most famous missionary in history, is buried in Westminster Abbey. Yet his own life was filled with growing pains. He wanted to go to China but had to go to Africa. Arriving on the field, he found conditions nothing like he had been promised. His relationship with other missionaries was stormy. A child died at birth and his wife was paralyzed. A lion mauled his arm and left him crippled for life. On top of that, his in-laws thundered with wrath at him for taking their daughter to Africa! It was out of this stuff that the world-famous missionary was molded.

Charles Spurgeon was the greatest preacher in the English language. Yet he preached out of the pain of intense personal suffering through gout and related diseases. His wife was an invalid confined to her room during the ten most productive years of his ministry. As the pained preacher sat in his wife's room one evening a log whistled in the fireplace. Gases trapped in the wood were released causing a brief, musical tone. Spurgeon told his wife Susannah, "It takes the fire to bring out the music." What is true of logs is true of life.

The following chapters deal with some of the fires that bring out the music. They tell you how to live at timberline. They will reveal the truth captured by the great prophet: "those who hope in the Lord will renew their strength. They will soar on wings like eagles; they will run and not grow weary, they will walk and not faint" (Isa. 40:31).

❧ *1* ❧

Rejection hurts . . . . It can come from family . . . peers . . . work.
And if we experience it repeatedly, it can cause us, no matter
how dedicated, to become depressed.

O Lord, you deceived me, and I was deceived;
    You overpowered me and prevailed.
I am ridiculed all day long:
    everyone mocks me.
Whenever I speak, I cry out
    proclaiming violence and destruction.
So the word of the Lord has brought me
    insult and reproach all day long.
But if I say, "I will not mention him
    or speak any more in his name,"
his word is in my heart like a burning fire,
    shut up in my bones.
I am weary of holding it in;
    indeed, I cannot.
I hear many whispering,
    "Terror on every side!
    Report him! Let's report him!"
All my friends
    are waiting for me to slip, saying,
    "Perhaps he will be deceived;
    then we will prevail over him
    and take our revenge on him."

Cursed be the day I was born!
    May the day my mother bore me not be blessed!
Cursed be the man who brought my father the news,
    who made him very glad, saying,
    "A child is born to you—a son!"
May that man be like the towns
    the Lord overthrew without pity.
May he hear wailing in the morning,
    a battle cry at noon.
For he did not kill me in the womb,
    with my mother as my grave,
    her womb enlarged forever.
Why did I ever come out of the womb
    to see trouble and sorrow
    and to end my days in shame?

But the Lord is with me like a mighty warrior;
    so my persecutors will stumble and not prevail.
They will fail and be thoroughly disgraced;
    their honor will never be forgotten.
O Lord Almighty, you who examine the righteous
    and probe the heart and mind,
let me see your vengeance upon them,
    for to you I have committed my cause.

                    Jeremiah 20:7-10, 14-18, 11-12

Defeating
Depression

Christians don't get depressed.

Do you believe that? A popular speaker has asked more than 100,000 Christians across America this question: "Is there anyone present who has never, ever, been depressed?" And the answer? Through all his speaking engagements, not one single person responded.

"Sometimes I'm up, sometimes I'm down / Standing in the need of prayer," the old spiritual goes. Do Christians get depressed? Of course they do. And they always have. From the writer of old spirituals to the spiritual giants of the Bible, Christians have struggled with depression. It is both an ancient and a universal problem. And very few people, Christian or no, have escaped its numbing effects.

There are several types of depression. Some people suffer from a chronic sort of depression, a clinical one caused by a malfunction of our brain's chemicals. Thankfully, modern medicine can now treat this sort of chemical disorder.

But the type of depression the rest of us suffer is the type the psalmist knew: "Oh, my soul, why art thou cast down within me?" he asked. History is littered with great people who have battled depression. Hippocrates described a state of mind 2400 years ago that he called "melancholy." Winston Churchill, the great statesman who led Britain during some of its crucial, modern times, suffered personally with a desperate "dragon of depression" that he feared would slay him.

But surely, the great spiritual leaders never had trouble with depression, did they? The easier question, after a close look at the Old Testament, might be to ask which leaders didn't! In reality, these strong Old Testament characters could easily be called the "miserable majority" when it came to depression. Moses, Elijah, Jonah—the list reads like a roll call of fame. Some of God's mightiest heroes who have proven themselves to be the most committed among us have struggled with periods of dark, desperate depression.

Read Numbers 11 and hear Moses cry out, "God, I wish You'd kill me! I can't bear leading these people any longer! All they do is grumble about how good the food was back in Egypt. Please just kill me!" Look at 1 Kings 19:4—Elijah, after his confrontation with the prophets on Mt. Carmel, rushes into the wilderness and cries, "God, just kill me! I've had it with this business of being a prophet!" Refer to the fourth chapter of Jonah where the prophet, strangely enough, is depressed because his "revival" was a big success. He didn't like God giving all those sinful Assyrians a second chance and asked God to just take his life. The more we look, the more we realize that depression is no respecter of persons.

The Depressed Prophet

But the worst case of all seems to be that of Jeremiah. From the chronicle he left us, his discouragement seems to be the rock-bottom depression of all time. Yet this is the prophet who was most often quoted by Jesus. No man in history could have possibly served God with greater integrity in more difficult circumstances with more complete surrender and undivided loyalty than the prophet Jeremiah. And yet this man was terribly, terribly depressed, as Jeremiah 20 shows us.

Jeremiah's book reads like a diary, the intimate papers or memoirs of a man called by God to prophesy. It's as if we are looking over his shoulder as he wrote about his innermost feelings. He seems to be writing to no audience but himself and God. And that perspective is very unusual, because it's something we don't get to do with any other prophet in the Bible. And maybe such an intimate angle is what makes Jeremiah's case so vitally alive, so vitally appropriate as we look for ways to defeat this devastating condition of depression.

The Reasons Why God's People Are Depressed

First, Jeremiah's "diary" can help us answer *why* we as God's men and women can succumb to depression. There are several viable reasons it can happen to any of us. Jeremiah's prayers in verse 7 of chapter 20 are almost painful to read, they are so open and personal, and seem so close to blasphemy. Jeremiah cried, "O Lord, you have deceived me . . . You overpowered me and prevailed. I am ridiculed all day long; everyone mocks me."

Literally, he says, "God, You entice me, You seduce me, You tricked me into being a prophet. And now for all these years, I have preached Your message and have gotten no response at all." Remember that Jeremiah had spent twenty years—two long decades—of his life proclaiming doom and destruction to his generation. *With no results.* So this prophet began to imagine "divine deceit." This discouraged man pointed his fingers at the heavens and in effect asked, "God, have You been a liar to me? Have You been like a river bed in the holy land, full of torrents of water during the rainy season, but now only a deceptive, dried-up river bed, a disappointment for a dry and thirsty man?"

This wasn't the first place Jeremiah prayed such a terrible prayer. Jeremiah 15:18 cries out with the same pain: "Why is my pain unending and my wound grievous and incurable? Will you be to me like a deceptive brook, like a spring that fails?"

Becoming depressed is easy when we imagine that God has deceived us. And if we are as honest as Jeremiah, we'd have to confess we've all looked up and made the same sort of remarks:

"God, I believed that if I married in the faith it would be like heaven. Instead it's turning into hell. Things haven't worked out like You promised."

"Lord, I've always lived like You taught us to live, been honest in all my dealings. Yet my life is in shambles. Things haven't worked out like You promised."

Or, "Lord, I thought if I gave You a tenth and put my finances in Your hands, everything would work out okay. But things haven't worked out like You promised."

We've all looked to heaven and imagined "divine deceit." If a spiritual giant like Jeremiah could fall into that trap, then how can we avoid it?

Repeated Rejection

But I think there was another reason that Jeremiah may have been so susceptible to depression. And it is one with which we are all too familiar ourselves. Verse 7 shows us this painful reason. "I am in derision daily," the New King James Version says. "Everyone mocks me." The emphasis here in the Hebrew is the idea that all day long people "whisper about me. They hold me in contempt. They deride me." Jeremiah faced *repeated rejection* from the people around him. Besides believing God was deceiving him, he believed the people around him were calling him names, rejecting him from every side, from across the entire nation.

Yet Jeremiah wasn't paranoid. They *were* whispering about him. When little children would see him in the marketplace, they would taunt him by saying, "There goes ol' 'Magor-Missabib,'" as it is in the Hebrew. "There goes ol' 'Death and Destruction.'" He'd hear from the men at the gates: "Look, here comes ol' 'Death and Destruction.'" He'd hear it in the marketplace: "Ol' 'Death and Destruction' is coming this way."

Jeremiah *had* been preaching about death and destruction—about violence and oppression—for two very long decades. That's not exactly the kind of message that wins friends and influences people. And so, the people began to deride him. Even his family plotted against him. In Jeremiah 20:10, the prophet writes, "All my friends are waiting for me to slip." He says, "All the men who say 'Shalom, Jeremiah, shalom,' whisper and rub their hands together as I pass, muttering, 'Just wait until he slips. Then we'll get revenge.'" But worse, his family was no better. When you read Jeremiah's biography, you find in the first chapter that his family actually plotted his death when he heard God's call to prophesy.

So, finally, maybe inevitably, all the rejection began to get to Jeremiah. He couldn't turn to family, to friends, or ultimately even to the Lord Jehovah. He experienced repeated, deflating, depressing rejection.

All of us can identify with this feeling in one way or another. We may never have had a whole nation whispering about us, but we know what it feels like to be rejected. It may go as far back as the playground. Whether it was being the last chosen for a team, whether it is being turned down for a job or ignored by someone you love, rejection hits hard—and the feeling doesn't go away for a long time.

I remember a fellow who lived down the hall from me in college—he was an expert on rejection! He was a good old boy but he had this problem with dates—he couldn't get one. He was turned down so many times that we all began to keep score. Then, finally, on the twenty-first request, some girl had mercy on him and accepted. We all laughed about it, even making a victory line as he went out the front of the dorm. But you know he was hurting. He'd been rejected twenty times, and it was public knowledge. It had to hurt.

Rejection Kills

Dr. Robert S. Elliott, an eminent cardiologist, was giving a lecture to a convention of his peers when he suffered a coronary right in the middle of his speech. Out of that experience, he wrote a book called *Is It Worth Dying For?* In his book, he records the impact and difficulty that can be caused by rejection. In 1965 he was sent by the U. S. government to deal with the highly skilled young men who worked at Cape Canaveral. It was a crucial time because the space program was being forced to cut back. After every space launch, the total work force was being cut by 15 percent. And these highly intelligent young men, some only 29 years of age, were literally dropping dead under the stress of not knowing if they were next to be rejected.

Rejection hurts, no matter what time of life we experience it, no matter where it originates. It can come from family, from peers, from social circles, from work. And if we experience it repeatedly, it can cause us, no matter how dedicated, to become depressed.

But surely a godly Christian can keep a tight rein on these feelings. Can't he respond rationally to those closest to him as he copes with depression?

Responses When God's People Are Depressed

Not if Jeremiah is a typical case history. Jeremiah *cursed* the day he was born, in verse 14. Instead of "Happy Birthday," Jeremiah was saying "Cursed Birthday." The Book of Leviticus states that it was a capital crime to curse your parents. And that's really what Jeremiah was doing! He was getting as close to blasphemy as he could without receiving capital punishment.

Such a response isn't that unusual. "I wish I had never been born!" Jeremiah might exclaim. I've had many people express such feelings to me more than once. Jeremiah was saying it. Depressed people will say it. And they all mean it. They do curse the day they were born. They'd rather not have been born than to go through this state of mind. The depression overwhelms them with an irrational feeling of unfairness. It's a natural response, and would be bad enough if it stopped there. But it doesn't. When we are coping with depression, we begin to react by being *irrationally* unfair to those around us. And that's even more depressing, especially to those closest to us.

Anger and Depression

Mortimer Ostow, a psychologist who deals with people suffering from depression, says that depression at every phase of its development includes a component of anger. And the anger is usually directed against the individual who is expected to provide love and support but who ultimately disappoints. This anger can force anyone on the verge of depression into responding in an irritating or hurtful way.

So depression cannot only make us darkly bitter, it can make us irrationally unfair, causing our own darkness to ooze out and touch the lives of others. When Jeremiah cursed the day he was born, he didn't stop there. In verses 15-17, he cursed the man who announced the news of his birth. And then he prayed that he wished the man had taken a sword and slain Jeremiah and his mother on the spot! That's a black and bitter response, if there ever was one.

What do you say to somebody like Jeremiah? "Oh, cheer up, Jeremiah, ol' boy. Things will get better"? I don't think so. He wouldn't believe it. And yet this is one of the greatest spiritual giants of our heritage?

I like what Martin Luther said about Jeremiah. He said, in essence, that those who say Jeremiah is not spiritual enough have never really experienced the stuff of real life and ought to keep their mouths shut. Jeremiah's depression didn't mean he was secretly a spiritual midget. Instead, it revealed a spiritual giant who still found himself experiencing growing pains. Even though the prayers found in Jeremiah 20 fall far short of the Sermon on the Mount, they come from the hurting heart of one of God's best, one of God's greatest servants of all time.

Resources When God's People Are Depressed

Surely, though, being a Christian should help in some way to get rid of such awful depression. Yes, it should. And it does. Through the pages of Jeremiah's "diary," we see what happens when a person of faith is knocked down by rejection, when he

imagines that God has let him down, when he experiences linger-
ing loneliness and alienation and then looks up and says, "God,
I've had it." And then it shows us how that person defeats his
depression. Verses 11-13 show a glimmer of hope. In these three
verses Jeremiah gets on top of it. He finds a way up and out of his
deep, dark experience, and we can too.

God Is Still Working

What were his resources? How did he get on top of it all?
First, he realized a very fundamental truth. *Even though God is
silent, He is still working in our lives.* Remembering that fact
is *Lesson Number 1* in defeating depression. But why, we want to
ask, why does He seem to be turning a deaf ear and a mute voice
to us? There are no easy answers to such a question. I imagine
Jeremiah had decided that God had closed shop and left town
after he had preached twenty years without any visible response.
Yet, slowly he found that God does work in silence.

We can see this truth in one of the last cries of Jesus on the
cross, which was followed by one of the most awful silences in all
history. Christ called out to God from the cross, "Eloi, Eloi, lama
sabachthani?"—words so striking that we have them recorded in
His native tongue: "Father, Father! Why have you forsaken me?"
At that moment, more than any other, Jesus needed a word from
God. And all was silent, deafeningly silent. Yet God was busier
than any other time in history, because during those six hours of
silence, God was actively redeeming the human race. And come
Sunday morning, God spoke loud and clear.

Depression comes easy if we begin to feel that God doesn't
have anything to say to us, but the first rule of defeating depression Jeremiah's way is to remember that God works in silence.

Keep Right on Talking

Lesson Number 2 is just as important, although it may seem
very hard to do: *Regardless of how bad things seem, never quit
talking to God.* There are prettier prayers in the Bible than

Jeremiah's. If I were going to write a sweet, daily devotional book of pretty prayers, I wouldn't choose these of Jeremiah. Colorful, yes. Honest and open, yes. Pretty? No.

But believe it or not, those harsh, angry prayers are what saved Jeremiah's life and ministry. Sounds crazy, but it's true. Because even as bad as things seemed to be, Jeremiah kept right on talking to God.

You may have never thought about it this way, but we do something rather strange—we talk about God behind His back, as if He weren't listening. We grumble and mumble about our own sort of "divine deceit." And just as we wouldn't talk to someone we felt had done us wrong, we rarely talk to God about our suspicions. So we talk about Him or around Him, but we usually stop short of actually talking *to* Him about the problem.

Instead of talking about God behind His back, though, Jeremiah had the grace to tell God exactly how he felt. And he found, as most of us can, that being open with God is one of the best ways to get-up-and-out of deep depression.

"But," you're probably worrying, "I can't rant and rave at the Lord Jehovah! What about lightning bolts? What about honor and humility?" Jeremiah didn't worry about those things. And we shouldn't either. Our relationship, our emotional and spiritual well-being, are at stake! Telling God how you feel won't make Him so dizzy He falls off His throne. He's taken on bigger and harder prayers than ours.

Over and over the psalmist told God everything that was on his heart. Job cried out the same way. And so did Moses and the rest. How will God react? Will He recoil at such impudence?

If you've ever been a parent, you no doubt remember the first time your baby threw a punch at you. In frustration and rage the baby lashed out, punching at the closest person. What did you say to that child? Did you scream, "You impudent little thing, I'm finished with you!"? Not likely. Probably you loved the baby all the more because of how tiny and fragile, how weak and helpless the baby was in its frustration and confusion. And that's how our Heavenly Father is with us.

Closing off ourselves from Him out of pride or anger or

self-pity will only grease our slide into deeper depression. Talking, even when the prayers are harsh, painful, even impudent-sounding, can help you overcome, just as it helped Jeremiah.

Reclaim the Promises

But there's one more lesson Jeremiah can teach us about defeating depression. *Lesson Number 3: Reclaim the promises and the praise of God.* Somehow, at his lowest, Jeremiah began to remember the promises God had made to him years before: "I will be with you." "They will not prevail against you." These were just two of the promises Jeremiah had heard from Jehovah. And as soon as Jeremiah began to recover the promises of God, he found, once again, the praise of God.

In verse 13, he began remembering all the good things God had done for him, all the times God promised to never reject him, to protect him. And he began to praise God for God's understanding.

We can do that—and we can experience the same change, because when we praise God for what He's done for us, we'll begin to remember those promises of God—to be with us always, to help us with our burdens, to show us the way.

I know this to be true in my own life. As a seminary student, I pastored one of those small village churches, and things seemed to be going well. Then, for some reason, I began to imagine rejection—even from the people I was working so hard to help! Looking back, I can see my depression was caused by that seeming rejection—just as it was for Jeremiah in a much larger way. But at the time, I couldn't see. My resignation shocked that little congregation. It was one of the worst experiences I have ever had. Almost everyone burst into tears, asking us what was going on and what was wrong.

As we packed our belongings into a little truck and pulled away, I was never so low in my entire life. I even decided to quit seminary after the semester was over. I intended to save my high grade average, but I went further and further down into depression and flunked exam after exam. I had never felt like this before.

Never had anything quite like this happened to me. In the middle of it all, someone told me I should stay busy, so I went out and got a job selling encyclopedias. And, believe me, that is not the job for anyone coping with rejection!

But somewhere down at the bottom of that awful experience, somehow through the grace of God, I learned that God was still there in my life. He was there, even through my disobedience, depression, and disappointment. Even my bad choices and feelings of rejection had not alienated Him. I realized that He wasn't through with me yet. And I began to praise God, thanking Him for the people in that little church who believed in me and trusted me. Then I followed that up with praise for everybody who had ever done anything good for me in my whole life. And slowly, somehow out of that experience, I was able to find the courage to ask that little church to take me back. And they did, with a unanimous vote—which was better than I did the first time around!

I know what it's like to sit where Jeremiah did. Most of us do. I also know what it's like to find my way up and out of that hole, to go on with Chapter 21 of my life. And most of us can do that, too. In the middle of that deep, dark, demonic depression, if you had told me that I would have had the ministry I've had in the last ten years, I would have just stared at you. And with a bitter, humorless laugh, I would have replied, "No way. I'm finished."

But I wasn't. Jeremiah wasn't. He preached for another twenty years and we find no record of any depression experience as debilitating as this one. And, even though it may be hard to believe while you're wrestling with your own black fog, you're not finished either. Whatever your reasons or your reactions, you can take three powerful lessons from Jeremiah's responses.

And, through the grace and wisdom of an understanding God, you can defeat depression and be on the "grow" again.

❧ 2 ❧

In the awareness of *His* control and our lack of it, I think,
we can alleviate our debilitating worry . . . .

"Therefore I tell you, do not worry about your life, what you will eat or drink; or about your body, what you will wear. Is not life more important than food, and the body more important than clothes?

"Look at the birds of the air; they do not sow or reap or store away in barns, and yet your heavenly Father feeds them. Are you not much more valuable than they? Who of you by worrying can add a single hour to his life?

"And why do you worry about clothes? See how the lilies of the field grow. They do not labor or spin. Yet I tell you that not even Solomon in all his splendor was dressed like one of these. If that is how God clothes the grass of the field, which is here today and tomorrow is thrown into the fire, will he not much more clothe you, O you of little faith?

"So do not worry, saying, 'What shall we eat?' or 'What shall we drink?' or 'What shall we wear?' For the pagans run after all these things, and your heavenly Father knows that you need them. But seek first his kingdom and his righteousness, and all these things will be given to you as well. Therefore do not worry about tomorrow, for tomorrow will worry about itself. Each day has enough trouble of its own."

Matthew 6:25–34

Winning
over Worry

Several summers ago, my family and I were on the Greek island of Naxos in the Aegean Sea. We had to take an eight-hour ferryboat ride through choppy waters to get there. The moment we set foot on the dock, though, we noticed a very strange sight. Everywhere we looked, there were Greek men nervously fingering strings of beads—worry beads, they called them. There were old men fingering worry beads, middle-aged men fumbling with worry beads, and young men fidgeting with worry beads. We saw them on the coast and we saw them as we moved farther into the interior of the island—worry beads were everywhere! The island was such a beautiful place we couldn't see what they all had to worry about.

Then an interesting thing happened. We wanted to take some sort of souvenir home with us to Texas—and we decided the only appropriate one would be worry beads. But the more we thought about it, the more we began to worry about what kind of beads we ought to get . . . .

31

There were different colors, different sizes, different strings that made different sounds. We were worrying about worry beads!

Everyone worries. It's the favorite American pastime. If we don't worry, we're probably worried that we aren't worried. And if we worry, we surely worry that we worry too much.

At the age of four, we worry about a dark room. At thirteen, we worry that we won't fit in at a party. As parents, we worry about our children.

The young executive, who has spent days preparing a presentation that will affect his future, worries what the boss will think. A factory worker reads of cutbacks in the defense industry and worries how it will affect his job.

All of us wrestle with worry. It's so much a part of our lives, so much a drain on our energy and attitudes, that Jesus devoted one-seventh of the Sermon on the Mount, the most famous sermon in history, to the subject. Evidently He believed that coming to grips with worry was of great significance for our lives. He devoted one word out of seven in this landmark sermon to how we can be liberated from it.

What do you think are the greatest concerns of living? Jesus recognized that we seem to be more concerned about the body that supports our life—what we'll put in it, what we'll put on it, and how we'll sustain it. But Jesus' response to these concerns is short, simple, and very, very true: We can stop our perpetual worry about these daily anxieties when we give ourselves to life's greatest concern—the reign and rule of God within us.

How is that so? To make His point very clear, Jesus gave us a command to heed, an argument to understand, and some illustrations to explain.

A Command to Heed

The command He gave us was this:

"Take no heed of what you will eat or what you will drink or what you will put on your body."

In other words, stop worrying about this "secular trinity" that we make so all-important. Three times in the Sermon on the

Mount He speaks of these three areas of life: what we will eat, what we will drink, and what we will put on. This materialistic trinity can consume all our thoughts.

If we kept a worry list for seven days, most of our worries would fall into one of these three basic categories. In King James language, we'd say, "Take no heed." Today, we'd say, "Quit being so distracted with anxiety." The word "worry" in the Greek means literally to tear apart, to distract, to come apart at the seams of a garment. And the grammatical construction Jesus used in these words tells us that the people to whom He was speaking were habitually, perennially, torn apart by anxious care. "Stop being so torn apart by worry over the basics of life," He was actually saying. It's not foresight He's prohibiting, but *foreboding*, not necessary preparation and planning, but constant, useless anxiety.

But it's all easier said than done, isn't it? Stop worrying! For many of us, that's like saying, "Stop breathing!" I read a little poem the other day. It went:

"I've joined the new 'Don't Worry Club'
And now I hold my breath.
I'm so afraid I'll worry
That I'm worried most to death."

An Argument to Understand

But Jesus must have understood that it's never enough to simply tell us to stop worrying. He didn't just give this bare command to stop being anxious about the basics of life, but He showed us how by giving us a very logical, spiritual argument. There is a secret, you see, to winning over worry. And that secret is grasping a "Lordly logic" . . . .

Let's examine the "Lordly logic" of Jesus. He said that God's greater gifts always include His lesser gifts, too. He seems to be asking three questions: "Do you believe that God gave you the great gift of life and that He gave you a body to sustain it? And did your worry have anything to do with that gift? And can your worry improve that gift?"

And then, He makes His point: "Is not life more important than food, and the body more important than clothes?" (Matt. 6:25).

Jesus often used a technique of teaching from the higher value to the lower one, and it never works better than it does here. The device makes us see the situation through His mind. We begin to see how futile, even silly, much of our worry is.

For instance, have you ever thought about this: when we were at the most vulnerable moment of our entire lives—those months before we were born—we not only didn't worry, we couldn't worry. And yet we were born. He gave us that gift of life. Why would He give us that greater gift if He were not going to give us what we needed to sustain it? God doesn't do things halfway. He's not that kind of God. Did you ever see half a mountain? Or half an ocean? He gave us a world full of life and eyes to see it. He gave us a world full of knowledge and minds to comprehend it. And as Romans 8:32 reminds us, "He who did not spare his own Son, but gave him up for us all—how will he not also, along with him, graciously give us all things?"

If God gave us that great gift, surely He can be trusted to sustain us with the basics of life for as long as we live. Job 14:5 says, "Man's days are determined." We must understand that fact. We don't know that number. But I believe God wants us to grasp that for the lifetime determined for us, He will give us everything we need for our bodies. In the awareness of His control and our lack of it, I think, we can alleviate our debilitating worry. Just a little readjusting of our perspective makes His Lordly logic ours.

Illustrations That Explain

We can see this truth in the Exodus story. When God liberated the Israelites from Egypt, that great gift of liberation also included the lesser gifts to make their liberation successful. Manna fell every day for all those years, water flowed out of the rock, a pillar of smoke led them by day and a pillar of fire by night. God took care of them.

And so He will take care of me. My worry has given me

nothing. God gave me everything, and He will always include the lesser gifts we need to sustain the greater gift.

The key word here, though, is "sustain." We live in a very affluent society, and often we can get our needs mixed up with our desires, don't we? This text is a wonderful promise. But it is not a promise to fulfill our desire to satisfy some society-bred greed. It's a promise to meet our *needs*. That's all. And there's a big difference. Jesus didn't say that we will feast, but He said, "you will be fed." He didn't say, "I will open up a charge account at Neiman-Marcus or JC Penney for you." In effect he did say, "Look at the lilies of the field . . . . Your Father in heaven takes care of lowly flowers. He will take care of you."

Americans have all kinds of fears. I recently read an article that reported how a thousand people responded to a poll of their ten greatest fears. The first one was death of a loved one. The second one was serious illness. The third was financial failure. Fourth was nuclear war, and fifth was fear of being a victim of crime. Do you know what number six was? Fear of snakes and spiders! One man wrote in to say that the Russians could place him in a room, release a couple of snakes, and he'd tell them anything. It's estimated that between two and five percent of all Americans live with constant, festering concern and fear—literally disabling phobias of one kind or another (*Psychology Today*, Dec., 1982, p. 84). This is to say twenty-five million among us are constantly battling some phobia. Agoraphobia, the fear of open spaces, alone affects twelve million in this country.

But the Lord is telling us that if we lock into His Lordly logic and realize that He will sustain what He's given, we have nothing to fear.

Look at the Birds

And knowing how effective illustrations are, Jesus gives us several to make His point even more vividly. He says, look at the birds. Worry for them is unnecessary. God is watching over them. The Greek word He uses is literally a command. "Look!" He commands. "Look closely at the birds." If we do, first we'll see that the birds are inferior to us. They can't sow, they can't reap, they can't gather. That is, they cannot plan or produce or store anything away for the future. They can't pray. But Jesus points out that our Heavenly Father feeds them. If you ever study an almanac, you'll read that one of the signs of a coming heavy winter is that the berry bushes will have more berries on them than normal. The birds are being taken care of. They will fare well even though they cannot plan, produce, or store away. And with His Lordly logic, Jesus asks in effect, "Are you not much better than they? If God so cares for the sparrow, will He not care for you?"

Of course, the cynic among us will point out the dead bird he saw the other day. But as mentioned earlier, our days are numbered; so a sparrow's days are numbered too. Jesus never said we wouldn't die. What He said is the sparrow doesn't have to worry while it's here.

I've always been fascinated with hummingbirds, so fragile, tiny, and beautiful. There are actually 320 kinds of hummingbirds. The Encyclopaedia Britannica tells us the tiniest among them is the "Bee-Humming" bird. It is 2 and $1/8$ inches long and half of that is tail feathers and beak. It only weighs five grams, just about the same weight as several aspirins would be in your hand. And yet that bird can hover, it can go up and down, sideways, and in and out with the most amazing grace and flexibility. It flaps its wings ninety times a second. And that little bird somehow knows that when it begins to get cold, for its own health it's best to leave far Northern Canada and migrate across the United States and the Gulf of Mexico, all the way to the Panama Canal Zone. And it knows when to turn around and go back. Just an accident? If you think so, you're the type who believes there could be an explosion in a printing plant and unabridged dictionaries would fall from the sky! Jesus points to the birds and says, "Look at God's concern for that small creature—and learn."

God cares. Even for little hummingbirds. And that means He cares for us. ⋅

Jesus' next point, in essence, is this: "Look at yourself," He says. "Which of you by worrying can add one inch to your stature? You can worry yourself to death, and you're not going to be the least bit taller." As always, Jesus' arguments speak volumes to any age, but this argument meant even more to the men of His time. In his book on *Luke*, Ray Summers says the average Jew in Palestine was only about five feet tall. And at that time, the land was occupied by Roman soldiers who were taller and much brawnier. So many of the Jewish men would spend a lifetime feeling upset because they would never be able to look their Roman captors right in the eye. So they felt the soldiers looked down on them. Jesus responded by stating the obvious—they could worry all they wanted to, but it wouldn't change their height one inch. He said, in effect, "Look at yourself. There are boundaries to your life, and worry will not change them. Accept that."

Sir Walter Scott, the great poet, lost all his money through a bad investment. He later lost his grandson and was told his wife had an incurable disease. His reply came from a Shakespearean play, *Henry IV*. He said, "Are all these things necessities? Then let us face them like necessities." Our Lord expects us to use common sense, to accept certain boundaries in our lives that worry will not help. So stop worrying about these matters. It's totally useless. Paul prayed and prayed for God to take away his thorn in the flesh. God didn't do it. So it became a necessity of his life, and he said, "Nevertheless, in my weakness I was strong." Zacchaeus was very short. Instead of feeling sorry for himself because he couldn't see over the crowd to see Jesus, he climbed up in the tree. He faced the necessity.

Look at the Lilies

And then Jesus cites His last illustration. "Look at the flowers. Why are you worried about what you will wear? Become a 'disciple' of the lilies of the field." That's literally what He meant. Make yourself a thorough disciple of the wildflowers. He wasn't talking about a pampered, hothouse lily. He was talking about the little flowers common all over Galilee. They were eaten by cattle, trampled by soldiers, even harvested and placed in little clay ovens where the people made their bread. Jesus pointed out that these flowers are only temporary. Consider them. They toil not, neither do they spin. Flowers don't even have the advantages of the birds. Birds at least can hunt and peck and migrate and build nests. Flowers just stand there. The most any flower can do is what the sunflower does—turn its head toward the sun in the morning, hold its head up high at noonday, and turn to the setting sun at the end of the day. Yet Christ said, "Pick out one of them, just one. Solomon in all his glory was never arrayed like the flower."

How was Solomon arrayed? A group of architects totaled up the cost of Solomon's temple as it is described in the Old Testament. Using all the gold, all the silver, and all the other precious building materials, they estimated it would cost eighty-seven *billion* dollars to build it today. And yet Jesus said, one wild flower is clothed in more glory than Solomon in all his glory.

Is the Lordly logic seeping in? Maybe we can believe it in our minds, but find it difficult to accept in our hearts. In other words, maybe we can't make the jump from believing the fact to getting rid of our worries. Yet if we can believe that God does sustain the gifts He's given us, then why don't we put that belief into practice?

"Oh ye of little faith," Jesus says over and over. Oh ye of pygmy, midget faith, He's saying. What can we do?

I remember a story that illustrates the answer wonderfully. One of those daring early pilots was circumnavigating the globe in his tiny airplane. Some 2,000 miles out to sea, away from any sort of land, he heard a gnawing somewhere under his cockpit. As he listened, he realized that it was a rat gnawing away at the wires and insulation of the plane. And he realized that he was in big trouble. What could he do? Then he remembered that rats are either subterranean or terrestrial creatures. So, he flew the plane a thousand feet higher, then another, and another until he was up to 20,000 feet. The gnawing stopped. When he reached the end of his journey and finally landed, he found a dead rat under the floor of his cockpit. The rat had been gnawing away at his very life line. But what did the pilot do? He found that when he lifted the whole situation up into another atmosphere, literally, the threat of the rat that was worrying him was removed.

Jesus says we need to move into another atmosphere—a calm, confident trust, the kind that little children have, toward the Heavenly Father.

Facing the Future

I can hear you say, "Well, I'm not worried about anything like that. I'm worried about the future." There's a degree of sophistication, it seems, in worrying about the future. Books like *Megatrends* and *Future Shock* keep us continually thinking about it. Movies like *Terminal Generation* can't help but make us worry. But here in the Sermon on the Mount, Jesus says, "Do not worry about tomorrow, for tomorrow will worry about itself. Each day has enough trouble of its own" (Matt. 6:34). The Lord makes this clear, concise promise: "I will sustain you in the worries and the concerns of a single day." You *can* master the demons of worry if you'll confine them to a single day. Absolutely. We must understand this . . . God Himself never promised that He would help us carry the guilt of yesterday, the burdens of today, or the fears of tomorrow. He said, "You put your guilt from yesterday under the blood of Christ, you give your anxieties about tomorrow to tomorrow, and I'll help you sustain yourself today."

In actuality, if you go to tomorrow to borrow worry for today, you're going to find the interest is astronomical. It just grows and grows. "I will help you live *today*," is what the Lord promises.

Poet Robert Burns had problems with alcoholism and depression. He battled all through his life with both. One day he saw a field mouse and wrote a famous poem, "To a Mouse," to it. "Oh, you wee, creeping, timorous beastie," he said to the mouse. "Thou art blessed compared with me, the present only touches thee. I look back on prospects drear/And I look forward at only guess and fear." He envied a mouse because a mouse has no choice. It lives in the now.

That's where God wants us to live. Several years ago, several ministers I know each returned from a partnership mission tour in Brazil with a stuffed piranha. Finally, after seeing several of these creatures placed strategically on their desks, I asked one of my friends what the ugly piranha's significance was. He explained, "One piranha may hurt you, but it cannot devour you. Piranhas only become lethal when they overtake you while swimming in schools."

The stuffed piranhas were a reminder that anyone can handle one worry at a time, one day at a time. And the Lord told us that He can help us handle the worries of a single day. We can master anxiety if we confine it to today.

And past today? Christ's ultimate cure for worry is this— "Seek first his kingdom and his righteousness, and all these things will be given to you as well" (Matt. 6:33). The bottom line when it comes to getting rid of our worries, our distracting cares, is simple. Substitute life's greatest concern for our little concerns. The tense of the verb "seek" is to keep on continually seeking the reign of God in your life as a habit.

When I was in junior high, we did an experiment with iron filings on a piece of paper. When we poured the filings on the paper they fell into a disheveled pile. Then we put a magnet under the paper and, as if by magic, the iron filings lined up . . . and followed the magnet's shape and force of direction. All our anxieties are like so many iron filings poured out on the surface of our lives. Jesus says, "Put My presence and My kingdom underneath your life, seek Me as a habit, and you'll find that your worries will line up and take My shape." The greater gift is given, and the lesser ones will be taken care of.

That's His promise, and our choice.

🌹 *3* 🌹

Jesus is my Advocate when I am overwhelmed by the guilt of my sin.

Blessed is he
> whose transgressions are forgiven,
> whose sins are covered.
Blessed is the man
> whose sin the Lord does not count against him
> and in whose spirit is no deceit.

When I kept silent,
> my bones wasted away
> through my groaning all day long.
For day and night
> your hand was heavy upon me;
> my strength was sapped
> > as in the heat of summer.
Then I acknowledged my sin to you
> and did not cover up my iniquity.
I said, "I will confess
> my transgressions to the Lord"—
and you forgave
> the guilt of my sin.

Therefore let everyone who is godly pray to you
> while you may be found;
surely when the mighty waters rise,
> they will not reach him.
You are my hiding place;
> you will protect me from trouble
> and surround me with songs of deliverance.

I will instruct you and teach you in the way you
> > should go;
> I will counsel you and watch over you.
Do not be like the horse or the mule,
> which have no understanding
but must be controlled by bit and bridle
> or they will not come to you.
Many are the woes of the wicked,
> but the Lord's unfailing love
> surrounds the man who trusts in him.

Rejoice in the Lord and be glad, you righteous;
> sing, all you who are upright in heart!

Psalm 32

Grappling with
Guilt

A story is told about an interesting prank pulled by the famous playwright Noel Coward many years ago. It is said that he sent an identical note to twenty of the most famous men in London. The anonymous note read simply:

"Everybody has found out what you are doing.

If I were you I would get out of town."

Supposedly, all twenty men actually left town.

What if you opened your mail one day and found such a note? What would race through your mind? Even though you've probably done nothing, it's a safe bet that, for a brief moment, your heart would beat a little faster and your palms might get a little sweaty. If you doubt it, think back to the last time you saw a police car in your rearview mirror. When the police car finally passed you, didn't you breathe a sigh of relief, and chastise yourself a little for those crazy, unfounded guilt feelings?

We all live with a great weight of false guilt and anxiety hanging over us. I don't mean the real and necessary sort of biblical guilt that helps us realize we're sinners and leads us to repentance. I mean the kind of guilt that dogs our lives, and that comes from who knows where and makes us feel miserable.

Some people never marry and feel guilty that they didn't; some marry and feel guilty that they did. Some never have children and feel guilty about that; others feel guilty about the poor parenting job they are doing with the children they have. Some sick people feel guilty over the care they are forced to receive from others; other healthy people who have sick people in their family feel guilty they aren't caring for them as they should.

We all carry around little guilt and big—about phone calls not answered, letters we *have* answered, books we've read, books we haven't read . . . and on and on.

The other day I listened to the actual recording of a psychologist's scheduled therapy sessions. One by one, several people came in and unloaded the guilt they felt.

One Jewish man shared his feeling of guilt because he was the only member of his entire family to survive a concentration camp during World War II. In another case, a woman expressed her guilt over being unable to appropriately care for her aged mother. She even felt guilty that she'd had to institutionalize her parent.

But we "normal folks" aren't much different. If I were to ask you to identify your guilty problems, you could probably list several things. And so could I. Some of our feelings would probably be well-founded, while others would be totally unfounded. Yet guilt can keep us from ever experiencing the fullness of life we as spiritual people should daily know. It can cripple us emotionally, mortally hindering our spiritual growth and keeping us from experiencing our full potential as people of God.

That sounds quite serious, doesn't it? Well, it is.

So, how can we get rid of this awful, draining guilt? We must begin to believe what the Word of God tells us about the reality of the Christian life. And a good place to start is Psalm 32.

Relief and Release

Of all people, David had good reason for feeling guilty. As we know, his sins were immense. Scholars believe that Psalm 32 was written by David as a twin to the 51st Psalm. Psalm 51 was written in the white-hot heat of David's cry to God for forgiveness over his double sin of murder and adultery. Most scholars believe that Psalm 32 was written sometime following the events which occurred after David had experienced the forgiveness of God. He had internalized that forgiveness, God had set him on his feet again, and the psalm reflects that experience. Relief and release from guilt are written all through it. "Blessed is he whose transgressions are forgiven, whose sins are covered / Blessed is the man whose sin the Lord does not count against him . . . ."

It's easy to see why Psalm 32 is called a penitential psalm. It was written to give the reader words to take to God.

As New Testament Christians, we have something even David, "the man after God's own heart," didn't have. John gives us a promise that can break the stranglehold of guilt on our lives: "If anybody does sin, we have one who speaks to the Father in our defense—Jesus Christ, the Righteous One" (1 John 2:1).

These two scripture passages hold the secret to overcoming guilt. Any of us can experience freedom from guilt if we do two things: 1) tell God like it is, and 2) turn to Christ as our Advocate.

Telling God "Like It Is"

Every Bible reader is familiar with David's amazing, terrifying, exciting story. It reads like fiction—but it's all true. David, the sweet singer of Israel, author of Psalm 23, chosen by God as king to replace Saul over Israel, aborted all that promise and potential in one sinful act—an act that led to more sin and more sin. One day he lazed about on the roof of his palace. Below him he saw a woman bathing, and he took her in adultery. Later on he had her husband killed to cover up his guilt. And then he covered his sin for more than a year.

Finally at the end of that year, he came to himself, with the help of Nathan, and confessed his sins of adultery, murder, deceit, and dishonor.

Why would such a story be included in the Bible? It shows us God's unconditional power to forgive. If God can forgive such heinous crimes and wipe a man's soul so clean he could write songs about it that would live for centuries, then certainly God can come to grips with my guilt and yours.

I believe the Scriptures also tell us how David went about getting rid of his guilt through confession. David seems to have understood confession better than anyone, maybe because he had sinned so deeply. But his actions show us how to make these principles workable and alive in our own lives. Based on three words David used to describe what he'd done, I believe his confession was three dimensional—Godward, manward, and inward. And I believe these are the three different dimensions of "telling God like it is."

Godward

First of all, there is the "Godward" aspect. The New International Version of the Bible uses the word "transgression." That word means, "I have rebelled, I have mutinied against God. I have openly revolted against the government of God in my life." It is the same word that was used in secular Hebrew of the Old Testament to speak of one king who had attacked another, one nation revolting against another.

Man in Revolt

Emil Brunner said that the whole human race could be called "man in revolt." When David came to his spiritual and moral senses, and began telling God "like it is," the first thing he said is, "Godwardly, I have rebelled."

He didn't say, "First of all, I have broken my own standard of conduct," although he had. He didn't say, "First of all, I have broken the trust of my great friend Uriah," although he had. First of all, he looked up to the throne of God, and, probably choking on the words, said, "I have rebelled against Your throne."

Until we can come to grips with this Godward dimension of "telling it like it is," of facing the cause of our guilt and dealing with the split between us and God, we will never be free of guilt's hold.

Manward

Second, let's look at the "manward" dimension. In Psalm 32, David says, "Blessed is he whose sins are covered." The word *sin* means "to miss the mark, to have your aim deflected." It is our failure to come up to the standard we have set for our daily lives. It is the very opposite of what Paul meant when he wrote, "I press on toward the goal to win the prize for which God has called me heavenward in Christ Jesus" (Phil. 3:14). In effect, David was saying, "Godwardly, I have rebelled, but manwardly, I have even missed the mark I set for my own life."

I have a feeling David was thinking about his amazing childhood. There was old Samuel anointing him to be the king of Israel as they both stood in a pasture. I'm sure David probably remembered the precious years he had spent with God as a boy, writing wonderful poetry and singing beautiful songs. And he probably thought, *I never intended that my life would turn out so marred—that I would break the heart of God and the trust of my friends. I have missed the mark in my own life.*

Manward (or womanward), we miss the mark in our own daily actions. We all set our own standards and when we do not live up to them, we heap guilt upon ourselves that clings and festers.

I have some long-suffering friends who decided seven years ago to teach me how to play the game of golf. I was almost thirty years old and they felt I had been deprived. So they invited me out on the golf course, telling me I could never be a minister of the gospel unless I learned how to play golf. I hadn't quite figured out the logic of that statement, but I figured if they had the patience, I had the time.

And boy, were they patient. I remember one friend laid down his #1 custom-made Ben Hogan driver parallel to me. Then he said, "I want you to swing your #3 iron right along that club and then through." So I proceeded to swing it right up the shaft so well that I hit the wooden head and broke it into a thousand little pieces. Well, my friend turned purple. Then he turned blue. But he didn't say anything.

Later, I was out with another friend. Thinking golf carts were like go-carts, I went driving up a hill and turned the cart and us over. After awhile, I was actually able to make contact with the ball. But that opened up a whole new set of problems. When I finally made contact, I found out that the ball just wouldn't go where I wanted it to! In fact, the harder I tried to make it go in one direction, the more it went in the opposite direction. Quickly, I learned that everything is opposite in the game of golf.

Isn't being a Christian the same? When we begin to get serious about following the will of God, we meet Christ. And for a long time, we just bungle everything. We can't seem to make contact with the will of God. But when we start making contact, we want everything to go the right way. But it just doesn't. And then we find what Paul said to be true: "For I have the desire to do what is good, but I cannot carry it out" (Rom. 7:18). We just miss the mark, the standard we set as men and women of God.

Inward

Third, there is the "inward" dimension. The King James Version uses the word "iniquity"—"whose iniquity the Lord does not count against me." The word "iniquity" means that there is something twisted in me that needs to be straightened out by the grace of God. There is something bent that needs to be unbent; there is something crooked that needs to be straightened out.

The other two words, "sin" and "transgression," deal with "doing." When I sin, I have rebelled against God; when I have transgressed, I have missed the mark. But "iniquity" is on the level of "being." Inside my being there is something that needs to be corrected. It is a collective thought. As David looked back over his whole life, he realized that, over all, his life was like a picture hanging crooked. He needed God to straighten his life's picture.

When we admit, as David did, in these three ways—that we've rebelled against God's government in our lives, that we've missed the mark, and that there is something crooked within us that needs straightening—then we have the capacity to feel clean as David did. Why? Because we can claim the promise David experienced.

And what promise is that? As Augustine, that great early Christian put it, David's words were no more out of his mouth than God had already forgiven him. God is just waiting for us to be real with Him. To tell it like it is. That's the essence of the phrase in verse 2 that says, "in whose spirit is no guile or deceit." God waited for David to stop blaming everybody and everything else and to simply make that three-dimensional confession.

Blaming everybody else? We don't know for sure what happened during David's year of silence, but I have an idea that he tried to deal with his guilt humanly during that time. Possibly he dealt with it as we might. He might have said, "Look God, it's Your fault. It's Your fault I happened to be on that roof and saw Bathsheba. You're in control of the universe. You must have set it up that way."

Does that sort of thinking sound familiar? That's exactly what happened in the Garden of Eden. The man blamed the woman. The woman blamed the snake. And they both blamed the fruit on the tree. But the problem wasn't the "apple" on the tree, but the "pair" on the ground. And so it is with us. And just as it was with David, no sooner is our confession out of our mouths than God has forgiven us of our sin and is able to deliver us from our guilt.

You notice I said that God is "able to deliver us" from our guilt. It is possible to confess our sins, be forgiven, and still be loaded down with our own burden of guilt. That's when guilt becomes false. And that's when the problem can become quite debilitating—not only spiritually, but psychologically and physically. You can actually make yourself sick.

Dealing with Guilt

If you don't deal with your guilt, then your guilt will deal with you. In his book, *Whole People in a Broken World*, Dr. Paul Tournier says that many people have come to his office complaining of all kinds of problems, some of them physical. Time after time, these symptoms would turn out to be nothing more than the expression of some repressed guilt from years before that had never been dealt with.

But 3000 years before Paul Tournier discovered the physical impact of guilt, David described it eloquently. "When I kept silent, my bones wasted away through my groaning all day long. For day and night your hand was heavy upon me; my strength was sapped as in the heat of summer" (Ps. 32:3).

Evidently, during that year David experienced some sort of illness related to his sin. His strength was sapped, he was feverish, and he lost weight. Physically, he was feeling guilt's effects.

And then David spoke of guilt's psychological effects. He said, "My conscience roared all day long. My mind was like a ravenous roar of a leaping lion and I heard it all along." That lion image goes all the way back to David's boyhood. As a shepherd boy he had lived out in the fields of Bethlehem in absolute quietness. All day long he heard only the low moan of the sheep. But sometimes, altogether unexpectedly, he would hear the roar of a leaping lion. At that moment, he himself had to leap into action to protect the sheep with his own life.

And then, as an older and guilt-ridden man, he could hear his conscience roar all day long. When he awoke in the morning, there it was leering and growling. At high noon, it roared, and at night, as he tried to sleep, it still rumbled. His mind was in absolute turmoil. This is one of the most vivid mental images David could use.

Other than the writers of the Bible itself, no one has so expertly pictured guilt as Shakespeare. He wrote that the mind of a guilty person is "full of scorpions." We may think our guilt has spent its force but when danger, death, or detection draws near, that guilt will revive.

Shakespeare's characters show the long-lasting effects of guilt: Brutus, guilt-stricken after killing Caesar, keeps seeing Caesar's ghost. Lady MacBeth sees blood on her hands after taking part in a murder. MacBeth seeing floating daggers.

Guilt.

Can this really happen? Can guilt really make us physically and mentally ill? Dr. Norman Covanish of the University of

California in Los Angeles has studied the subject for decades. In 1968, he did an interesting series of investigative studies of single-car accidents on the Los Angeles freeway system. Reviewing hundreds of cases (about 1 ½ percent of the total) he found that 25 percent, one out of every four, was very definitely caused by the driver acting out self-destructive behavior because of guilt.

One woman, for instance, early in her marriage had been caught in a felony. When her husband found out, he told her that if she ever did anything like that again, he would divorce her. Years later, she embezzled some money at work. Her boss threatened to tell her husband. When she left work that day, instead of going home the usual way, she took another route. In a moment of self-destructive guilt, she went over the side of a hill in her car. She survived and explained what guilt had caused her to do.

Dr. Covanish says when we live with guilt year in and year out, these same self-destructive impulses will surface, whether it's behind the wheel of a car or in a myriad of other ways. David himself was on the way to utter personal ruin.

So the truth is that if you don't deal with your guilt it *will* deal with you.

How, then, do we deal with it? We must begin to believe what the Bible is telling us. We must believe that what happened to David can happen to us as well. And then we must turn to the advocacy of the Lord Jesus Christ.

Our Guilt Is Gone

We've seen the beautiful words that David used in the Psalm: his transgressions were forgiven, his sin was covered, his iniquity was not counted against him. He reminds us that the same God who covers the sky with blue in the day and inky darkness at night, also covers the meadow with wild flowers in spring and snow in winter. This same God covered David's sin— his and ours. "My iniquity he does not count against me." God has not written down our sins anywhere. They are gone— eradicated. And we need to believe the reality of that fact.

Computer technology has given us a good modern example of this truth. A few months ago I was in Birmingham, Alabama. I had slaved over twenty-four pages of a book I was writing on James. It was tough. For days I had entered and stored information on the computer's diskette. Then one afternoon, I went down to get a cup of coffee in the hotel dining room and there was some kind of surge in the power of the hotel. When I got back to my computer, my work was gone! Vanished. I became so excited I called the computer salesman in Fort Worth. I said, "Where did it go?"

He said, "Nowhere."

I said, "It's got to be somewhere. All that work—it was on there!"

He said, "It's nowhere."

I said, "Isn't there any way of getting it back?"

And he said, "No, never."

That's exactly what God did for David. When David told God "like it was," suddenly his sin and guilt were gone—gone forever.

But we should understand that principle even better than David does. David looked back on a temple made of stones, but we look back to Calvary. David looked at animal sacrifices— bleating bulls, yapping goats—while we look back with 20/20 hindsight on the only begotten Son of God who was slain to obliterate all our sins—and our guilt.

And so if David believed that his sins were covered and lifted and erased, and that his life should be guilt-free, then how much more should we?

Turning to Christ as Our Advocate

To truly be capable of ridding our lives of guilt's hold, as Christians we must take seriously the promise in the King James Version of 1 John 2:1—"If any man sin, we have an advocate with the Father, Jesus Christ . . . ." Literally, we are having Him *now*. Whenever we need Him, He is there. John doesn't say we will have an advocate if we sin, when we feel bad long enough. He said we *are having* an advocate—always.

"Advocate." The word means Jesus is literally face to face with the Father in our behalf. David knew nothing of that relationship when he wrote Psalm 32. Yet he knew the truth innately. We have a powerful Advocate in Jesus Christ.

Think about it. The name Jesus should remind us of that very position. His name Jesus means that He is a sympathetic Advocate. That's His human name. When Jesus was born, the angelic messenger said, "You are to give him the name Jesus, because he will save his people from their sins" (Matt. 1:21). But His name is also Christ. That is His name of power.

I have many friends who are sympathetic toward me, but they can't help me. They may say, "Hey, you blew it, or hey, I'm sorry," but beyond that, they cannot help me at all. But that name Christ means that Jesus is the anointed Son of God—the righteous one, as John goes on to describe Him. And this means He has the power to stand before God for you and me, because He needs no one to stand before God for Him. "I owed a debt I could not pay," the old saying goes. "He paid a debt He did not owe."

Jesus is my Advocate when I am overwhelmed by the guilt of sin.

Many people misunderstand Christ's advocacy role, however. Jesus doesn't go up to the Father and say, "Well, now, it's true that Joel Gregory down there didn't strictly tell the truth today. And it's true that he didn't go exactly where he was supposed to go. But look, he's a pastor and a writer and an all-around good guy. . . . That ought to count for something." That's not the way it works. The thought here is that there is a kind of balancing of the books. Jesus pleads something of merit over and against my sin.

Nothing could be further from the truth. Jesus does not hold up my petty little "goodness." Instead He says, "Gregory has missed the mark. He's rebelled against Your authority and government. There's something crooked in him that needs straightening. But I want to remind You, Father, what I was sent to do for him. I left heaven to go down to earth to keep Your law perfectly for 33 years. Then on that cross I substituted a crown of thorns for a crown of glory—for him. I was mocked for him. I bled for him. I covered him from head to foot with My perfect living, and

My perfect dying. And because of that, I know You will forgive him, Father."

That's what it meant to know the forgiveness of the Lord Jesus Christ—to trust the realness, the utter dependability of His advocacy, and to believe we are forgiven. That is the only possible way for us to know freedom from guilt. Until we allow the reality of our Christian lives, the power of Christ's gospel, and the Word of God to address the dilemma of guilt, we *cannot* be free of that burden.

Tell God like it is. Then believe in Christ's wonderful advocacy. When you rely on these foundational Christian truths, you *can* be free from guilt.

 4

If we do not learn to dwell in the secret place of the Most High,
to abide in the shadow of the Almighty, the years to come are
going to fill our hearts with increasing fear.

He who dwells in the shelter of the Most High
will rest in the shadow of the Almighty.
I will say of the Lord, "He is my refuge and my fortress,
my God, in whom I trust."

Surely he will save you from the fowler's snare
and from the deadly pestilence.
He will cover you with his feathers,
and under his wings you will find refuge;
his faithfulness will be your shield and rampart.
You will not fear the terror of night,
nor the arrow that flies by day,
nor the pestilence that stalks in the darkness,
nor the plague that destroys at midday.
A thousand may fall at your side,
ten thousand at your right hand,
but it will not come near you.
You will only observe with your eyes
and see the punishment of the wicked.

If you make the Most High your dwelling—
even the Lord, who is my refuge—
then no harm will befall you,
no disaster will come near your tent.
For he will command his angels concerning you
to guard you in all your ways;
they will lift you up in their hands,
so that you will not strike your foot against a stone.
You will tread upon the lion and the cobra;
you will trample the great lion and the serpent.

"Because he loves me," says the Lord, "I will rescue him;
I will protect him, for he acknowledges my name.
He will call upon me, and I will answer him;
I will be with him in trouble,
I will deliver him and honor him.
With long life will I satisfy him
and show him my salvation."

Psalm 91

Security —
Will God Protect Me?

Scared to death.

There's enough in this world to scare us to death, isn't there? But did you know that you can actually, literally, be scared to death? As recently as 1980, studies have verified that people can literally be frightened out of their lives (*Science Digest*, Nov./Dec., 1980, p. 105).

A prominent scientist examined fifteen cases in which people, four of them children, were assaulted. They could not flee and they could not fight, so even though they received only minor injuries, they died. They were so afraid, it seems, that they were actually scared to death.

How is this physiologically possible? Upon examination, the evidence indicated that stress caused by fear had literally destroyed the victims' hearts. Heart cells were destroyed by the body's violent reaction to fear, said the study. Because the people were utterly helpless, they couldn't fight back and they couldn't escape, their adrenalin kept on pumping into their hearts, and their hearts, overwrought, destroyed themselves.

We live in a scary world. And the impact of the fear we live with is real and deadly. I remember a cartoon in *The New Yorker* several years ago in which an elderly apartment dweller was in the process of locking the seven different locks on his door—deadbolts, sliding locks, security locks. All the time the blade of a saw was cutting a circle in the floor under him! It was a humorous attempt to make a serious point. There really is no possible escape from everything that threatens us in our world. That is why the words of Psalm 91 are more poignant today than ever.

Someone has said that Psalm 91 is an expanded commentary on the great cry of the apostle Paul: "If God is for us, who can be against us?" (Rom. 8:31). What is the message of the Psalm? Its message is a promise for God's people in an increasingly frightened and insecure age. It's a promise we must take to heart in today's world—or live our lives in fear and timidity.

The Promise of Protection

And what is that promise? God promises us shelter, covering, and comprehensive protection based on His very nature. Those who claim the promise and dwell in the shelter of the Most High will rest in the shadow of the Almighty. God offers us security, says the psalmist, by providing secret shelter.

In the first verse of the psalm, we find the act of faith, the steps we must take. What we must do is search for that shelter. And then we must be willing to use it. What does that mean? To dwell in that shelter is continually to commune with God, reposing our trust in Him, depositing our confidence in Him. The psalmist says that the promise of security is for the individual who is willing to do this. But it is an act of faith to dwell in such a way. And this keeps many of us from ever experiencing that special treatment.

But why do we shy away from this act of faith? Because we know that being a Christian doesn't keep us from harm. It doesn't keep us from death and accidents and illness and pain and crisis. So it's hard to understand fully what "protection from God" could be if we still experience such danger.

Yet let's look at what kind of protection this promise calls forth from God. If we make the choice to dwell in His secret place, as the psalmist puts it, then God's response will be to treat us as His guests. In the ancient eastern world, the duty of the host was the most sacred duty a man could have. Even to this day, if you come into the tent of a Bedouin or another nomadic desert dweller, he will protect you with his very life. This is the background from which the psalmist was writing. Almighty God is saying, in effect, "When you dwell in My most secret place, I promise to be your divine host with the sacred responsibility of covering and caring for you." When we deposit our trust in Him, then He guarantees He will give us His sheltering protection against all that harms us— *until our duty is done and our race is finished in His service*.

We will still go through trials. That is part of life. But the psalmist says we can go through these trials with confidence. If we are "dwelling" in communion with God, if we are accepting the shelter only He can give, then we will be safe until our work for the Lord is over, until our time on this earth is done.

How does this protection work? I believe He protects and secures those of us who take that step of faith to dwell with Him in several very interesting ways.

Look back at the figure of speech used by the psalmist. He speaks of a God who covers us with "His wings."

"He will cover you with his feathers, and under his wings you will find refuge." The reference is to the great wings of an eagle as they stretch out to stabilize the young eaglet in flight—or to cover it if it tumbles from the nest while trying to fly. The very first word that God spoke to Moses on Mt. Sinai was to remind Moses that He brought the people out of Egypt "on eagle's wings." Think of it. The God of the cosmic universe—of unfathomable, immeasurable space—that great God condescends to relate to us like an eagle who spreads out its wings to protect its young.

On Eagles' Wings

I can't help but think of an enlightening article I read recently. It was written by several noted ornithologists and described the time they spent watching one family of eagles nested on the edge of a canyon. As they watched, the eaglet hatched and grew. On the sixty-seventh day, the little bird stood on the edge of the nest for an hour and a half, then stretched its wings trying out the air, testing its tail feathers, leaning forward into the wind over the canyon's edge. Suddenly there came the mighty moment when the eaglet's legs pushed off the nest and, for the first time, it tried to fly. The result was almost disaster. Some little kites hovering around the canyon's edge began to divebomb the little eaglet. And the eaglet lost control so completely that it was about to crash into the wall of the canyon and fall to its death. Then, just at the right moment, the father and mother eagles flew down to the eaglet and surrounded him, one on either side. Flying in formation beside it, the parents allowed the eaglet to use the thermal currents their wings were causing to help itself stabilize. Then they escorted the eaglet back to the nest.

This is exactly the picture the psalmist is painting of God's promise to us. God is there, to come alongside us. How often do we dive off into dangerous situations, half prepared? Then when we're about to crash, we find that the goodness of God is there, stabilizing us, enabling us to find our way home. This is the great promise in Psalm 91. The God whom we meet in Christ not only promises us a hiding place but He promises to stabilize us like an eagle with its eaglet.

Enter the Angels

But if we read further, we get the rest of the promise. The psalmist tells us that when we put our faith in that security, God actually protects us through angelic intervention. That's right. Angels.

Do you believe in angels? No, I'm not talking about leprechauns or munchkins or muppets—or fairy tales. Do you believe there are beings created to serve God and do as He bids? The psalmist states with certainty that God will command His angels "concerning you to guard you in all your ways. They will lift you up in their hands so that you will not strike your foot against a stone." The Modern Language Bible says, "He gives his angels orders regarding you, to protect you wherever you go."

Do you believe in angels? The Scriptures clearly state that God uses supernatural beings in His government and providence of the world. So, on the basis of the Word of God, we have no more reason to doubt the existence of angelic protection than we have to doubt the existence of Abraham or Moses or Paul—or even Jesus Christ Himself.

The Bible tells of "cherubim and seraphim," angelic beings that protect the children of God "in the way." When he sent out a servant to seek a bride for Isaac, Abraham was told, "My angel will go before him and show him Rebecca." The Lord God promised Moses that the angel would go before him in the Exodus. In Second Kings, Elisha's servant was fearful of the gathering army so Elisha prayed that God would open his eyes. Suddenly Elisha saw the chariots of the host of heaven. The birth of our Lord was announced by angels and then attended by them. Christ was ministered to by angels in the wilderness and in the Garden of Gethsemane. And angels were in His empty tomb, announcing His resurrection. Hebrews 1:14 promises that by angelic protection God leads His children along.

The evidence is there. But what do they do? This psalm seems to indicate that they exercise vigilance, guarding us in all our ways. When Satan used part of this reference to angels to tempt Jesus, he omitted those last words—"guard you in all your ways."

It still seems hard to believe, doesn't it? But the promise is that as long as you walk in the way of duty and fidelity to God, until your "race is run and your testimony done," He will, even by angelic interposition, guard you. And the psalmist goes on to say that not only will angels guard you, they'll also lift you up. The original Hebrew literally says, lift you up "on their hands"—lifting you up over the impediments and difficulties of life.

Angelic Intervention

I believe this happens. I can cite many true stories that support my belief. I think about one in particular. A prominent nineteenth century clergyman had gone to catch a train in New York on his way to a speaking engagement. He said he stood on the train platform, tranquil, anticipating the ride. Yet as the train pulled up, he said he was absolutely riveted to where he was standing. He tried to lift a leg to get on the train, but could not move a muscle. "I was conscious of an overwhelming force forbidding me and hindering me to move," he explained. As he stood there stupefied, the train pulled out. Two miles down the track, the famous Revere train accident happened. Scores of people on that very train he could not board were killed instantly. The only way he could explain it was that he was conscious of an angelic force in his life because his work in this life wasn't done.

In his book *Angels: God's Secret Agents*, Billy Graham recounts many such instances of secret, spiritual forces giving protection.* One story he told I had heard personally from some of the people involved in it. One tragic night in China, bandits had surrounded one of the mission compounds that sheltered hundreds of women and children. On the previous night, one of the missionaries, a Miss Monsen, had been confined to bed with a malaria attack. She worried herself all night long with questions such as, "What will you do when the looters begin firing on the compound? What about the promise you've been trusting in and the witness to these people you're trying to win to Christ?"

So Miss Monsen prayed, "Lord, I've been teaching these young people all these years that Your promises are true. And if they fail now, my mouth will be forever closed and I must go home."

Throughout the next night, she was up and about, ministering to and encouraging the frightened refugees and orphans. And though fearful things happened all around the mission

---

*Adapted from *Angels: God's Secret Agents* by Billy Graham (Waco, Texas: Word Books, Publisher), 126–127.

compound, the bandits left the compound untouched. In the morning, people from three different neighborhood families asked Miss Monsen who the four people were, three sitting and one standing, on the top of her roof the night before. Miss Monsen told them that no one had been on the housetop, that in fact, it wasn't even accessible. But the neighboring families refused to believe it. They said they had seen these strange beings with their own eyes.

Of course, you can draw your own conclusion. But the conclusion the missionaries came to was that in this remarkable situation where the Christian faith of weak, young believers stood at risk, God interceded in a remarkable way.

The Names and Nature of God

In whatever way God chooses, He wants us to have that ultimate assurance of protection. And we can be sure of it for one very good reason—because of His *nature*. That's the ultimate reason why we can believe in it. In the first two verses of Psalm 91 there are no less than four names given for God. The psalmist speaks of God as the "Most High." He is a God who is inaccessible in His height above all difficulty and danger, yet He is *there* for His children. Let everything rage that can rage on earth beneath. God is Most High.

Second, the psalmist speaks of God who is Almighty—His great Hebrew name is El Shaddai. It's the name on which Abraham leaned as he walked into the unknown. Nothing is powerful enough to overcome Him because He is God Almighty.

Third, He is called Jehovah. That is His covenant name, the one that means "I Am That I Am" or "I Will Be What I Will Be." "I can outlast anything that threatens My people," the name is saying. And *that's* an amazing promise.

God is also described by the psalmist using the personal pronoun, "he." At this point theology moves into testimony. Instead of talking about an impersonal God, the psalmist moves into personal confession. "He is my refuge, my fortress, my God, in Him I will trust."

It will do you little good to read these words about a God who gives His people protection and then set the Book down and go on. Just reading it is not enough. What leashes us to that protection is the act of "cleaving" to it, leaning on it in trust, saying not just that there is a God, but that He is "My God, my refuge, my fortress. In Him I trust." When theology becomes testimony, when observation becomes confession, that's when we can have the experience this psalmist did.

Delivered from Danger

But we spoke of danger earlier. How does this protection keep us from the danger we feel all around?

We can divide everything that threatens us into two big groups: *obvious* dangers (those we can see approaching) and *unexpected* dangers (those that blindside us). One thing about this psalm is that the psalmist does not leave God's protection generalized. He becomes very specific about it. He says God can protect you from open, obvious, manifest danger as well as the hidden, secret, insidious type. "Surely He will save you from the fowler's snare," the psalmist exclaims. "You will tread on the cobra and you will trample on the serpent."

The fowler's snare was a kind of net set up to catch unsuspecting birds. This and the poisonous cobra waiting to strike are, of course, metaphors for all the traps waiting secretly for us. He, El Shaddai, the Most High God, Jehovah, can keep us from those secret snares.

And then the psalmist says, "You will tread upon the great lion and trample upon the serpent." For the Hebrews, the ravenous lion was an open, obvious threat. But we're no different. We live with our own kind of "leaping lion." *Psychology Today* tells of an emerging epidemic in which middle-aged people suddenly are simply afraid to drive. Even though they've gotten up and driven to work for years, these same people cannot face the open places where they have to drive anymore. Drunken driving, widespread abuse of speed limits, smaller and smaller cars, and larger and larger transport trucks have made them feel the odds are stacked against them.

But the psalmist says, "You will not fear the terror of night." We won't feel the kind of nocturnal dread that comes from sudden attack.

Then he speaks of the arrow that flies by day and the plagues that destroy at midday. These are open, obvious, manifest attacks.

"But a thousand shall fall at your side and ten thousand at your right hand, but it will not come near you." God's people, the psalmist is saying, should not fear danger. As long as their duty is not done, until God's plan for them is completed, they will stand unscathed. It's like the passover in Egypt when the death angel passed them by—or the Red Sea when the waters piled high for them and flooded back down on Pharaoh's army. The psalmist assures us that this is not just an Old Testament truth, it is God's truth for everyone who deposits faith in the Most High.

This reminds me of a story about General Douglas MacArthur. Over and over, believing himself a man of destiny, MacArthur demonstrated his ability to stand while others cowered around him. In 1943, a naval admiral assigned to MacArthur to work with amphibious warfare thought the general arrogant and didn't like him very much.

One day MacArthur invited the admiral to join with him in the first wave of an assault. The naval admiral knew he must go, but he wasn't prepared for MacArthur. As they stood on the beach, the admiral could not take his eyes off the general—uniform resplendent, khakis sharply creased, brass polished—standing there straight-backed with shells bursting all around him. Then, MacArthur asked the admiral to stand beside him in a picture he wanted taken. The admiral couldn't believe it, but he stood for the picture with MacArthur. Just as the picture was taken, a shell fell a few yards away and everybody hit the sand—almost everyone, that is. The admiral, the photographers, and everyone else looked up from the smoke to see General MacArthur still standing erect. "Why are you all on the ground?!" MacArthur asked.

We cannot help but admire people with that kind of courage. But few of us have that quality.

The average American, according to *U.S. News and World Report* (Dec. 12, 1983, p. 72), runs a higher risk of being a victim of a violent crime than of being hurt in an auto accident. I read and reread that statistic. While you are reading these words, 690 serious crimes will take place (*U.S. News and World Report*, Oct. 27, 1980, pp. 58f.). During a thirty-minute period, 375 thefts, 180 burglaries, 66 violent crimes, 25 robberies, 4 rapes, and 1 murder will take place. The survey said that Americans are paralyzed by fear of one another. And I think we are all coming to understand that there are not enough security systems available, not enough money to hire police, not enough locks to put on our doors to keep away every kind of threat that can come our way.

If we do not learn how to dwell in the secret place of the Most High, to abide in the shadow of the Almighty, the years to come are going to fill our hearts with increasing fear.

Yet questions still haunt us. What about the accidents and the illnesses and the pain that Christians must endure every day? What about the deaths of fine Christians we all know about? I want to give you the answer that John Calvin always gave to such questions. He said, "When we look back on our life, from the perspective of eternity, we're going to see that the power of Satan was so great, that the weakness of our flesh was so feeble, and that the hostility of the world was so strong, that every day of our life—if God had not intervened—we would never have made it through a day" (Calvin's Commentaries, Vol. 5).

We have God's protecting providence every breath we take. It is a promise offered to us, but it is up to us to believe it and live it. Sometimes it seems that trust cannot hold out, that *we* cannot hold out. The psalmist closes with just that thought. God is telling us that we don't *have* to hold out. He's saying, in effect, "I'm the one who holds out, and My very Name is at stake here." El Shaddai, Jehovah, the Most High—He is powerful, above all dangers, and is the God of covenants that He keeps.

Our security does not rest in our weak, feeble, timid, fragile, finite humanity—not for a moment. Our security is in clinging to a God who takes care of those who take the conscious step of faith to believe.

❧ *5* ❧

Ours is an imperfect world and imperfect things happen. And we
are not exempt . . . because we happen to believe . . . .

Consider it pure joy, my brothers, whenever you face trials of many kinds, because you know that the testing of your faith develops perseverance. Perseverance must finish its work so that you may be mature and complete, not lacking anything.

James 1:2–4

Testing—
Handling Life's Tough Times

Life's tough times. Every day in one way or another we all face "trials and tribulations" of varying size and significance. How do we react to them?

Some people react with denial. "This isn't happening to me," they say—and bury their heads in the nearest sand.

Some people react with escape. They smoke a joint of marijuana or snort a bit of cocaine or have an affair. Bars are full of people who are trying to drown their problems with alcohol.

Others react with a shallow kind of optimism. I heard about a Sunday school class in which every week each member was asked to share his or her favorite verse. Invariably one man would always stand and say, "My favorite verse is 'Grin and bear it.' It's in the Old Testament somewhere."

And then there are those who react to life's troubles with pessimism. You know them. Every time you see them, they're singing a different verse of "Nobody Knows the Trouble I've Seen."

Is there a better way to react? Should a Christian respond

differently than someone without faith—in a way that would help his soul to grow?

James says there is a better way. "Consider it pure joy . . . whenever you face trials." James wants us to know in no uncertain terms that we can face life's tough times with a sense of confidence—even joy, believe it or not—if we understand God's purpose in the trial.

There's probably not a more practical message than this one James gives us. First, James obviously wants us to recognize the reality of life's testing times. He does not say *if* you face trials. He says, *when* you face trials. Becoming a Christian is not like getting a free pass through troubles. Those who preach such an idea are far off the mark. The truth is, as we've discussed earlier in this book, we probably face *more* trials because of our commitment to Christ.

Tough Times Are Inevitable

In fact, in his first letter Peter told the believers to stop thinking that the "fiery trial that has fallen on you" is strange and foreign. It's just part of life.

It may be a blister on your finger or an aneurism in your artery. It may be that you've lost your wallet or your business! It may be that you have your plans for a day ruined, or your hopes for a lifetime crushed. But the only guarantee is that tough times will come.

Then James, after pointing out that trials will definitely come, also points out that they come at inopportune times. They're lurking around the next corner to take us by surprise. In God's omniscience and providence, there's a day circled on the calendar when a test will come your way. The very language of this suggests their uncertainty. The King James Version of the Bible speaks of temptations, but the word in the Greek New Testament, "pirasmas," also means trials. In fact, it's the word from which we get our word "pirate," and that suggests the very nature of trials as James mentions them. They come like pirates, attacking us suddenly at indefinite times. It's the same word used in the Good Samaritan parable about the man attacked on the road to Jericho. We fall into the midst of these trials, ambushed by them. Life thumps along okay, God's in His heaven and all's right with our world, and suddenly we're face to face with troubles.

And then we can take the idea one step further. Not only do they definitely come, not only do they come at indefinite times—but they also come inconclusively. We get tests of all kinds. James says, ". . . when you face trials of many kinds." The Greek word for "many kinds" is a word that means "multi-colored." We will face variegated tests, tests of every hue and shade. It's the same word used in the Old Testament for Joseph's technicolor coat of many colors. I think that means two things. I believe it means that life's tests are personalized and that they are synchronized.

What do I mean by that? First, I think tests are "custom-made" for each of us. What may test you may not test anybody else. We can see that in the ministry of Jesus. Jesus didn't give the same tests to everyone. In fact, to several individuals He gave tests that were unique to them. To the rich young ruler, He said to sell everything the man had and follow Him. Christ didn't say that to Nicodemus or the woman at the well. Life's trials are personalized. And I think it helps us to have more sympathy with one another when we understand that fact. What may make another tremble might not even touch me.

But life's tough times are also synchronized. In other words, they sometimes come all at the same time. In the parable of the two builders, for instance, the rains pounded on the roof, the winds howled against the walls, the foundation of one house crumbled—and it all happened at once.

One of my favorite lines from Shakespeare is the line that says trouble seldom comes as single sentrymen, but usually comes as a battalion. When it rains it pours. You know it's true. We've all seen it. Tests of health lead to tests of wealth. These lead to emotional tests that in turn lead to domestic tests—and on and on.

Some Days Are Like That!

Recently I read a story about a young man in Utah who woke up because the plumbing in his ceiling was leaking and water was hitting him in the face. Jumping out of bed he found that the water was already ankle deep on his floor. The man decided to call the landlord. The landlord told him to go rent a water vacuum quickly and get the water up before it ruined his property. So the young man rushed out to his car and found he had a flat tire. He decided he'd better call for some help, so he ran back into his apartment, sloshed back through the water, picked up the phone, and it shocked him so badly that he ripped the phone off the wall.

By that time he knew he really needed help so he decided to go back down to his car. But when he tried to get out the door, the door wouldn't budge. The water had made it swell in its frame. So he had to scream from inside his apartment until some-body came and kicked the door down from the outside. He rushed out to his car only to find that somebody had stolen his car while all this was going on. He remembered it didn't have but a very little bit of gas in it, so he ran a couple of blocks down the street and there it was right in the middle of the road. Some people helped him push the car back to his apartment. Finally he got the water turned off, the flat fixed, and gas put in his car.

By that time, he had to hurry to make it to his ROTC gradua-tion ceremony. Grabbing his bayonet, he threw it into his car and ran upstairs to dress. When he ran back down to his car, he forgot that he had left his bayonet in the driver's seat. And he sat down on it. Minutes later, he found himself in an emergency room get-ting strategic surgery.

Trudging back to his apartment, he opened the door, and saw that falling plaster had toppled onto his pet canary's cage, killing the bird. As he dashed over to where the cage lay, he slipped on the wet carpet and injured his back. Once more he found himself in the emergency room. And by that time, a newspaper reporter had caught up with him. The reporter asked, "How can you explain a day like this?" The only thing the young man could say was, "Well, it looks like God was trying to kill me but He just kept missing."

Maybe you've had one of those days. Maybe you've had a month or a year like that. I think it is strategic to a solid Christian understanding to know that we will experience such times.

But I also think it's just as important for the Christian to look upon these events as growth experiences. We *can* see them as James sees them, however unreasonable that sounds.

"Consider it joy . . ." Joy? The word for joy here gives the idea of unmixed, undiluted joy. Christians are to face life's testing times with a rare, redemptive reaction. We shouldn't try to escape or deny them with bitterness or complaining or grumbling. Rather, we should consider testing as a training ground for further growth.

The model we have for this sort of reaction is our Lord Himself. The Scriptures say that Christ, "for the joy set before him, endured the cross, despising the shame." Jesus could even endure the test of the cross with this attitude.

Journey toward Joy

Don't misunderstand James. He doesn't mean "joy" in the sense of life's trials being your life's greatest joys. He's not talking about a "jump-up-and-down" kind of joy. The most mature believers I know don't hilariously go to the hospital or frolic their way through funerals or zestfully watch their bank account vanish to zero. That's not what James has in mind. The meaning is deeper.

The Word of God says the "joy of the Lord is my strength." James is not speaking of a superficial kind of merriment. He is speaking of the joy of the Lord—an inner sense of well-being that nothing, absolutely nothing, in life can touch. This sort of joy resides in the heart of every born-again and Spirit-filled believer. It is the inner assurance that even when everything around us has been shaken, we still have a confident relationship with God which cannot be touched. In this sense the joy of the Lord is our strength.

How do we get this sort of joy? James tells us that our outlook determines our outcome. Our viewpoint, our vantage point, determines our victory. The first word, "consider," gives us that insight. We must consider now how we will face life's tough times. Before we encounter troubles we need to decide how we are going to face them.

Why now? A smart camper doesn't wait till the storm comes to anchor his tent. If I have learned any lessons through almost two decades of pastoring, one of the major ones is that the time to decide how you will respond to life is not during tragedy. If we do not decide beforehand, we are at the mercy of life's trials.

Tested by Fire

Several years ago my phone rang in the middle of the night. The house of a young seminary couple who were members of my church had caught fire and was burning to the ground. So I made my way as quickly as I could to the house. The street was blocked with emergency vehicles, firetrucks, news camera crews, and floodlights. As I made my way up to the house, somebody told me that it was too late. The husband had rushed back into the house to rescue their new baby and had never come out. I was told that the wife had been taken to the hospital emergency room. As I drove there I had no idea what to do or say. Here was a young woman who had lost everything. What *could* I say?

When I found her, she was sitting in one of those areas with drawn curtains, her face soot-covered. Before I could say anything, she looked up at me and said, "Pastor, the Lord is the strength of my life."

This young woman did not decide at that moment to view life in that way. Obviously, it had been her practice for years to say, "The Lord is the strength of my life," and mean it. When she most needed that strength, it was there.

Everyone of us needs to come to a sort of "continental divide" in life. We may stand on one side for years, never having made a decision about how we will face life's little irritations and big tragedies. But when we reach the other side of this spiritual divide, we have made the decision that will shape the way we handle the rest of life.

It's also somewhat like crossing an international dateline. On one side it is one day, but when you get to the other side, it is another—another untried day with a brand new outlook. James says we must make that spiritual decision, we must cross that continental divide, that dateline, and firmly entrench ourselves into this spiritual way of viewing life.

Choose You This Day

What will happen if we don't "consider" and choose this attitude? Through life's little irritations, we will become perpetual grumblers, grumbling ourselves and those around us to death. And then when life's big trials come, we will be totally undone, totally incapacitated.

How then do we get to this point? By sheer willpower? I don't know too many people who can actually do that. It's as we mentioned at the beginning of this chapter. We can face the trials of our lives with confidence when we understand God's reason for allowing testing in our lives.

"Consider it all joy, because . . ." James says. He gives us an explanation. I can write over every test of my life a single, simple significant word. I can inscribe it over every trial I face—and that word is "permitted." God permits these trials.

I can hear you now. Does God burn down houses with seminary students and infants inside? Does God cause accidents and plane crashes? Does God throw hurt after hurt into our lives? No, I don't believe so. All these things are part of the natural law of the natural world in which we live. Ours is an imperfect world and imperfect things happen. And we are not exempt from such happenings because we happen to believe. But as believers we *can* write the word "permitted" over them. And when we do, we begin to understand how God works through that small, simple word.

Just as the strongest and most prized fish are those that struggle and leap upstream, so it is with our own struggles. We must go against the flow—and when we do, the struggle in our lives produces characteristics that change and shape us. They push us to make choices—growth choices. No pain, no gain, athletes say. It's true in the spiritual world as well. And it all begins with allowing ourselves to place the word "permitted" over life's tough times.

What do life's trials tell us about ourselves? What can we learn from them?

Genuine Faith

First, I believe that the testing we go through demonstrates the genuineness of our faith. In the phrase "the testing of your faith," the word "testing" is an almost untranslatable word. The Williams version explains it as showing what is "genuine in your faith." The idea refers to iron ore that has gone through the refining fire and comes out the other side clean and pure and genuine. This is the word Job used when he said, "When he has tried me in the fire, I will come out like gold."

Actually, there may be something suspect about a faith that has never been tested. An army going through basic training is not ready for battle. Not until soldiers have faced the battle, and been under fire, do they consider themselves proven, hardened, worthy. A ship cannot prove that it's been sturdily built as long as it stays in dry dock. Its hull must get wet; it must face a storm to demonstrate genuine seaworthiness. The same is true of our faith. When we hold fast to belief in Christ in spite of life's storms and crushing criticism, that's when we demonstrate the genuineness of our faith.

Durable Faith

Second, life's tough times reveal the durability of our faith. ". . . The testing of your faith develops perseverance," James assures us. Perseverance. Steadfastness. Endurance. Triumphant tenacity. Unswerving fidelity to the cause of Christ. To persevere is to "keep on keeping on" when life knocks you down. It's the ability to get back up and press ahead. God wants us to have that quality in our lives. If every day was a downhill slide with the wind at our backs, we wouldn't persevere, because we wouldn't know how to do it. That's why it took Joseph thirteen years to get from the pit his brothers threw him into, to the palace of the king. That's why Moses spent forty years in the wilderness before returning to lead the Israelites another forty years. That's why it took Abraham a hundred years kicking clods in the Holy Land waiting for clear direction from God.

When we ask, "Why is this happening to me?" one very good reason is that it will develop the grace of perseverance in our lives. Jesus counted perseverance so significant that He used the same word in Mark when He said, "Whoever perseveres to the end shall be saved."

To put it another way, we not only have a gospel of the good start, but we also have a gospel of a good finish. Too often we forget to talk about the importance of finishing the Christian walk.

Can we believe that our trials are actually doing us a favor? That God is permitting these things in order to prove, to strengthen, to solidify the genuineness and durability of our commitment? When I look back on my own trials, I am certain of one thing. If I have any Christian maturity at all in my life, most of it has come because of the tough times in my life, I wouldn't trade what I learned on the mountain peak for what I learned in the valley.

If we understand the words of James to his fellow first-century Christians, we as Christians can turn our irritations into edifications, our trials into triumphs. We can quit being victims of the things that happen to us. There *is* a way to consider it all joy. And that is through this special "joy of the Lord." Only someone who understands the *purpose* of testing can know what this means.

6

King Saul . . . was aware of his abilities and gifts . . . . (They) made him think he could begin to make life's biggest decisions without waiting on God.

. . . When Samuel caught sight of Saul, the Lord said to him, "This is the man I spoke to you about; he will govern my people" (9:17).

. . . When Samuel brought all the tribes of Israel near, the tribe of Benjamin was chosen. Then he brought forward the tribe of Benjamin, clan by clan . . . . Finally Saul son of Kish was chosen. But when they looked for him, he was not to be found . . . . And the Lord said, "Yes, he has hidden himself among the baggage."

They ran and brought him out, and as he stood among the people he was a head taller than any of the others. Samuel said to all the people, "Do you see the man the Lord has chosen? There is no one like him among all the people."

Then the people shouted, "Long live the king!" (10:20–24).

. . . The people then said to Samuel, "Who was it that asked, 'Shall Saul reign over us?' Bring these men to us and we will put them to death."

But Saul said, "No one shall be put to death today, for this day the Lord has rescued Israel" (11:12–13).

Saul was thirty years old when he became king, and he reigned over Israel forty-two years.

. . . Jonathan attacked the Philistine outpost at Geba . . . . The Philistines assembled to fight Israel, with . . . soldiers as numerous as the sand on the seashore . . . . When the men of Israel saw that their situation was critical and that their army was hard pressed, they hid in caves and thickets, among the rocks, and in pits and cisterns . . . . Saul remained at Gilgal, and all the troops with him were quaking with fear. He waited seven days, the time set by Samuel; but Samuel did not come to Gilgal, and Saul's men began to scatter. So he said, "Bring me the burnt offering and the fellowship offerings." And Saul offered up the burnt offering. Just as he finished making the offering, Samuel arrived, and Saul went out to greet him.

"What have you done?" asked Samuel . . . . "You have not kept the command the Lord your God gave you; if you had, he would have established your kingdom over Israel for all time. But now your kingdom will not endure; the Lord has sought out a man after his own heart and appointed him leader of his people, because you have not kept the Lord's command" (13:1, 3, 5–11, 13–14).

1 Samuel 9–13

Hidden Weaknesses —
The Sinkhole Syndrome

One day a few years ago in Winter Park, Florida, Mrs. Owens heard a strange sound outside her window. When she looked out, she saw her poplar tree disappear into the earth . . .

There in her front lawn—where there had been solid lawn—was now a huge hole, one that was getting bigger by the second.

Before that sinkhole finished growing, it had swallowed Mrs. Owens' three-bedroom home, five neighborhood cars, the deep end of the town's municipal swimming pool, and a solid block of land. The hole was as long as a football field and eight stories deep.

Can you imagine it? If there is anything we take for granted it is the firmness of the earth under our feet. But the "terra firma" under Mrs. Owens was suddenly somewhat less than "firma." How could that happen?

Beneath that city block were limestone caverns, once filled with water but now dry. When the caverns were filled with water they were solid. But something had siphoned off the water, and when that hidden water was drained away, houses, cars, businesses, and streets sank down and out of sight.

81

Though we may not believe it, we can be victims of a certain sort of sinkhole ourselves. We may never have our house fall into the earth, but we might easily watch our lives fall uncontrollably into a sinkhole of their own. It makes no difference how gifted we may be personally or how much we have accomplished individually. If we are not careful, the sinkhole syndrome can swallow us up. In fact, there is a good case for believing that the more we accomplish, the more gifted we are, the easier it is to fall into the syndrome.

Searchlight on Saul

This awful possibility is no more clearly demonstrated than in the life of one distinct biblical man, a man who had perhaps more natural gifts and higher personal achievements than any individual up to his time—King Saul, the first king of Israel.

Saul was tremendously gifted. He had an outstanding home on the towering hill of Geba and a fabulous heritage as the son of the affluent Kish. He was even physically striking, being the tallest man of his generation—which would be quite an advantage during that time for a leader.

But he also had the gift of divine intervention in his life. His life seemed almost charmed.

One day he left home to look for some lost donkeys, and he wandered into Samuel who recognized him immediately as the man whom God had designated to be king. Young Saul went out to find donkeys and found his destiny instead. That would be like a farm boy from rural Britain wandering around Westminster Abbey until all of a sudden the Archbishop of Canterbury grabs him and crowns him King of England.

But then Saul also had the gift of religious experience to add to his list. He experienced a miraculous demonstration of God's activity in his life. Saul, of course, expressed disbelief at Samuel's sudden and strange announcement. So to convince the young man that he had been chosen king, Samuel told him that he would encounter two men who would tell him where his donkeys were. Then he would meet two men who would hand him two loaves of bread. And then, ready or not, when he returned home, young Saul would actually see two prophets descend from the "High Place" and the Spirit of God would come on him. Then Saul would join the prophets in ecstasy and praise to God. Samuel even told Saul that God would alter his heart.

And all of this happened exactly as Samuel described.

Add all of these prophetic advantages to Saul's character as a leader, and we have a picture of one who seemed truly ordained, chosen and set apart for very special things.

And when Saul began to lead, he did seem too good to be true. It's one thing to be crowned a king, another to act like one. And Saul took to it naturally. As a leader, he was innately strong. For instance, Israel wanted desperately to have the Ammonites' protection on the east bank of the Jordan River. The tribes there were very tempted to succumb to the pagans' demands in return for the much-needed help. But when the Ammonites' leader said his army would only give the protection if his soldiers could blind every Hebrew man's right eye, thirty-year-old Saul became so righteously angry that he tore an oxen into parts, sending them to all the twelve tribes of Israel. He threatened to do the same to their oxen if they didn't band together with him to defeat such a sadistic pagan.

Yet he also had compassion on those Israelites who opposed his leadership, sparing their lives. Over and over, we can see his gracious statesmanship, outstanding creativity, and leadership abilities—all innate gifts. Saul was even humble. He actually hid "among the baggage" when lots were cast for his kingship. He had to be literally carried out to be crowned king. In other words, Saul was the type of man every dad dreams his daughter will marry—a man of heritage, achievement, gifts, statesmanship, and leadership.

Yet we know the end of his story.

Saul's Sinkhole

Saul fell deep into his own personal sinkhole. He had every advantage and he still fell into ruin. How and why did it happen? And most importantly, can it happen to us?

The sad answer to the last question is yes. Saul's life shows us that we may have remarkable religious experiences, and we may encounter demonstrations of God's power that propel us ahead. We may be born with every conceivable advantage, and yet none of these can insulate us from the danger of the sinkhole. We often have the mistaken idea that such gifts and such religious experiences make the person who receives them "better" or at least different in a spiritual way than the rest of us. But it just isn't true, as the reality of the sinkhole signifies. No one is immune to life becoming a sudden spiritual sinkhole. How does it happen?

Remember what we said earlier about the nature of sinkholes? Everything looks firm and solid until the hidden strength, the waters, drain away from the underground, hollow caverns. No one can see it happening or know when those hidden resources are gone, but when they are dry, everything quickly collapses.

That was Saul's dilemma. He was relying on all those gifts, those advantages—on his own inner resources—to get by, and everything was fine for many, many years. Then, Saul's attitude began to make a difference.

We see that change in attitude when Jonathan, Saul's son, impetuously attacked the Philistines, and the Philistines retaliated. But the bulk of the Hebrew army ran, totally disappeared, vanishing deep into the limestone caves of the hills of Judea. Samuel had told Saul that before he did anything he should wait seven days until Samuel could join him. As a priest, Samuel would make an offering to God concerning the situation.

Here is the turning point in Saul's life. Saul waited, and on the seventh day when Samuel did not arrive, the remaining army began to scatter.

At that moment, Saul must have begun to feel fear. Because of his impatience, he lost his trust in the way that God had been handling his life so far. And he must have allowed his own pride, his own feelings of self-confidence to color his thinking. At that point Saul took matters into his own hands—he offered the burnt offering himself, taking on the role of priest without the counsel of God. And just as he finished, Samuel arrived.

When Saul went to greet him, Samuel said, "What have you done?!"

Saul had made an important decision without waiting for God's direction through Samuel, God's chosen messenger. So Samuel said, "You have not kept the command the Lord your God gave you. If you had, you would have established your kingdom. But now He has sought out another man."

Does that sound harsh? Yet Saul's downfall wasn't due to this one incident. There was something in the heart of Saul all the days of his reign that was slowly, surely draining the limestone caverns of his sinkhole. And it had taken this long to become apparent.

You see, Saul was an impetuous man. He was aware of his abilities and gifts. And all his gifts and achievements and advantages made him think he could begin making life's biggest decisions without waiting on God.

Our Modern Sinkhole Problem

Today, we often stand in awe of people who have such gifts and advantages, and we often envy them. As Americans we tend to believe that such brash, self-confident power is immensely attractive. Yet isn't it interesting to think that being so talented, so self-sufficient, so seemingly powerful can be the very cause of our spiritual sinkholes? Sometimes our very advantages can be a hindrance to spiritual guidance and long-term excellence.

Most of us have certain talents and advantages on which we rely heavily. We may even survive on them for a while. We may even go so far as to choose our educational and career goals on the strength of our talents—without truly seeking God's direction. Impetuously we may lurch forward in life without actually waiting for God's insight. Using our own innate intelligence and experience, we blindly move ahead toward an unknown future.

But Saul's story gives us a different perspective. Tragically, Saul demonstrates how the sinkhole syndrome can swallow any person's life if he or she makes a habit of not waiting on God for direction in absolute obedience.

As we know, God allowed Saul to remain in power, but the disobedient king made more and more headstrong mistakes. And his real finale, when he was swallowed fully by his own sinkhole, was his direct disobedience to God in dealing with the Amalekites told about in 1 Samuel 15.

The Amalekites were a blood-thirsty group, a sensual, insidious people who were like a cancer on the country and God's people. God told Saul to exterminate them, to obliterate them. God did not want one of the Amalekites to survive, not even their animals. As if He were a surgeon excising all of the cancer, He wanted not one malignant cell left to multiply and fester again.

What did Saul do? He went to the city, set up an ambush, and then, contradicting the call of God, he took Agag the king of the Amalekites alive. He also spared the best sheep, cattle, and fatted calves and lambs. In his own wisdom Saul decided what was good and worthy and then spared it. He then decided what was despised and weak and destroyed those animals.

When Samuel arrived on the scene, he could not find Saul. And then he heard a sound, a sound he should not have heard— the sound of sheep bleating. The men standing nearby denied hearing anything, but Samuel soon found the Amalekite sheep, plump and choice, tied close by. And Samuel knew Saul had gone too far. Saul's sinkhole had not only made him lurch forward in life without direction from God, but now, finally, it had pushed him into arrogantly deciding he could disobey God's specific command.

Then to that heresy he added hypocrisy. When Samuel confronted Saul, the king explained that the soldiers had brought the finest sheep and cattle back to the camp to sacrifice to the Lord God as soon as Samuel had arrived. All the rest they had destroyed as they were told, Saul explained piously.

Saul stands at the bottom of his sinkhole—a hypocrite lying to Samuel, the man of God. And at that moment Samuel turned on him.

Samuel said, "Does the Lord delight in burnt offerings and sacrifices as much as in obeying the voice of God? To obey is better than sacrifice and to heed better than the fat of rams." All God wanted from you, Samuel is saying to Saul, is simple obedience, not gifts or excuses.

How does the sinkhole syndrome cause the collapse of a gifted life of achievement? When does it begin to crumble the terra firma of our spiritual lives?

When we decide we are above simple obedience . . . that is the blunt answer.

How often do we rationalize, saying such things as, "I know that God wants me to commune with Him in prayer, but I've got a busy schedule. My day is full"?

Or, "I know that God wants me to be an obedient believer, committed to His church and its service. You don't understand the pressure in my life."

Or, "I know that God wants me to keep myself morally pure. I know I should avoid lustful and adulterous thoughts. But you don't understand the kind of world we live in."

One by one we begin to excuse ourselves for disobeying the commands of God. And we disobey them in arrogance and in pride and then in hypocrisy, as if we are serving God as we go.

This is the point at which our personal sinkhole caves in.

We may not even be aware that our sinkhole is growing bigger and bigger and we're sinking deeper and deeper into it. Making a habit of ignoring both our small and large disobediences, we rely more and more on our own resources. Thus we sink slowly, surely into our own holes, never noticing until we hit bottom. None of us are immune. That is why I call these subtle failures "hidden weaknesses."

One of the saddest contrasts in the Old Testament is the beginning words of the life of Saul and the last words we read about him. After such a wonderful beginning, Saul ended his days paranoid, afraid of life and afraid of himself. Finally, Saul tells his own armor bearer to draw his sword and kill him. When the soldier refuses to do it, Saul falls on his own sword, a suicide on the field of battle.

Lessons from Saul

How often do we see such defeat happen to seemingly fine, upstanding Christians? The more well-known they are, the more shocked we are when they succumb to a sinkhole experience.

Yet I think Saul's story makes it abundantly clear that sink-holes may happen *especially* to those of us with inner strengths and abilities and outward gifts and advantages. We are given such gifts for a purpose, a purpose that should continually keep us in tune with God's direction for us.

A very wise woman once said that she didn't worry so much about the devil working on her weaknesses—those she was well aware of and watched closely. Instead, she had learned that Satan worked more on her strengths, because in her strengths was the possibility of smugness, of self-assurance and rebellion against God.

Saul's story makes it clear that sinkholes are everywhere. They can happen to anyone. The multi-talented or the one-talented, the rich or the famous, the shy as well as the reticent. What, we should ask, is filling up the hidden caverns that lace our foundation? How much are we relying on our wit, our charm, our knowledge, our piety, our righteous standing in the church and community. How much do we depend on our power and privilege to get us through life?

Reliance on ourselves at the sacrifice of reliance on God can slowly yet surely crumble away our seemingly strong foundations. Saul's story tells us we are only as strong and firm as our commitment to God's leading—every single day of our lives.

7

There is holy amnesia and practicing it is one of the healthier
ways to keep our souls growing.

———— Not that I have already obtained all this, or have already been ——
made perfect, but I press on to take hold of that for which Christ
Jesus took hold of me.

Brothers, I do not consider myself yet to have taken hold of
it. But one thing I do: Forgetting what is behind and straining
toward what is ahead, I press on toward the goal to win the prize for
which God has called me heavenward in Christ Jesus.

Philippians 3:12–14

Releasing the Past — Holy Amnesia

A leading women's magazine (McCall's, Oct. 1986) recently carried the story of a thirty-nine-year-old mother of four who suddenly suffered a splitting headache. Before she knew what had happened, she was undergoing surgery for a brain aneurism. The operation was successful but had an unusual side effect. Partial amnesia caused her to forget sixteen years of her life. In her mind, she was twenty-three, the mother of four small children. Can you imagine the courage and patience it took for her to overcome that kind of experience? She'd forgotten all those years of happiness and achievement. But isn't it interesting to realize that she had also forgotten the hardship and the regrets of those years, too?

Some of us might think it would be a blessing to forget some of the things that have happened to us. Wouldn't we like to forget some of the things that we've done, things we're not proud of, things that keep haunting us?

In a spiritual sense, the apostle Paul would agree, but he'd also probably say that we might be better off as Christians if we would forget some of our *achievements,* too.

Does that sound strange? Paul spoke of wishing for a sort of "holy" amnesia in which he would be able to forget both the guilt of past failures (that could paralyze him) and the pride of past achievements (that would hinder his pace in the spiritual "race" he was running). So what does Paul say? "Forgetting both things, I press on."

In his letter to the Philippians, Paul makes it quite clear that growing believers should confess a kind of holy discontent with their spiritual growth. Often we allow one of these two things to keep us from continued growth—either we are paralyzed by guilt from the past or we are content through the pride of our past achievements.

Think of one experience from your past that you feel guilty about. Just one. Most of us have many to choose from, but one is potent enough to keep us down. We may even believe that God has forgiven us, but we just can't forgive ourselves. Our memory becomes an enemy and slows our pace in the spiritual race. We're slowed to a crawl, as if we're having to drag this mighty weight behind us every step of the way. And yet we do this to ourselves.

Now think of one experience from your past that you are proud of. Just one. Most of us upstanding Christians have many to choose from, and this list is not one we'll usually hide. Pinned on our mental bulletin board, we have that list out front so we can remind ourselves again and again how upstanding we truly are. Yet believe it or not, even one of those experiences is as potent as a guilty memory in slowing us down on our way to that goal of Christian maturity. How? We're so busy patting ourselves on the back for how far we've already come that we aren't concentrating on what's still ahead. And we may be quite content with right where we are. Again, our memory becomes an enemy in our quest toward wholeness in Christ.

Paul knew these two kinds of memory were deadly to spiritual growth. And Paul's own life is a great example of the possible effects that both sides of this memory coin can have.

To Brag, or Not to Brag?

First, Paul certainly had a lot of accomplishments to brag about, didn't he? Religiously, he probably had as many bragging rights as anyone who ever lived. And yet he was the first to point to his spiritual imperfection. In fact, he uses the word "perfect" in a strange way to describe himself. As he put it, he has not been "made perfect."

What does that mean? As evangelicals, we believe that the work of Christ *for* us on the cross was a perfect work—but we must confess that the work of Christ *in* us through the Holy Spirit is an imperfect work in that it is not yet complete.

Why? It's not because Christ or the Spirit is imperfect, but because we are. Paul made that clear in his own life. He said, "It is not that I already obtained all of this, or have already been made perfect, brothers. I do not consider myself yet to have taken hold of it." So Paul confesses a discontent, a dissatisfaction with his own spiritual progress, even though his credentials were absolutely impeccable. A lesser person would have been sitting on his laurels.

Think about Paul's situation. Here was a man who by this time had suffered imprisonment for the cause of Christ, who had founded churches all over Asia and parts of Europe. Here was a man who'd written the letter to the Romans, the greatest treatise on Christian doctrine ever written. Yet he's saying he had not obtained perfection. He had not grasped *the goal* of the high calling of Christ. Like a child standing by the seashore with the waves lapping at his feet wondering what the entire ocean must be like, Paul feels discontented, wanting to see more.

But let's look at the rest of Paul's bragging rights. Even before his conversion, he had a great deal to brag about. He tells us of his blue-blood background, of his orthodox upbringing, of his perfect education, and his card-carrying membership in the very elite group called the Pharisees. He was a Hebrew of the Hebrews.

Then after his conversion, he could have bragged how his family disowned him and his friends snubbed him. He had also suffered physically for the faith. He then continued down an unparalleled list of achievements as one of the greatest disciples of all time. Yet, he said, "I consider all of these things rubbish, that I might gain Christ. I press toward the mark for the prize."

Startling, isn't it? If we'd been put in prison for spreading the gospel, wouldn't it be somewhat difficult not to mention that sacrifice as quite a spiritual coup for us personally? How many of us wouldn't be proud if we had written Romans? Yet as Paul looked back on his entire Christian life, deliberately, fully, cautiously reflecting on it, he said, "I do not count myself to have apprehended the fullness of Christ." He had not achieved the maturity that a Christian ought to have.

Since he was writing to the Christians at Philippi about this situation, it's probably fair to guess that maybe some believers in that church were resting on their past achievements. Gnostics did believe that if a person kept the law of God perfectly, he or she could have absolute righteousness on earth—that spiritual perfection was possible on this side of the resurrection. And, of course, believing that, it would be only natural to keep quite a list of one's personal accomplishments, wouldn't it?

But are we that much different now? I have no doubt we know ourselves to be far from Christian perfection. Our difficulty may be that we haven't arrived—yet we're satisfied anyway. And smugness will remove us from the race toward spiritual growth faster than anything.

At the time of this writing Paul could easily have felt he had arrived. He had put in years and years of service. He could have pointed back to those early years of daring enterprise, those middle years of great responsibility, and sat back in smug satisfaction feeling retired with honor and distinction in Christian service. He could have had the attitude we see so often exemplified in the church today. But instead, he was making big plans. The impulse of his heart, the beat of his pulse was to get out of prison and take the gospel all the way to Spain. He literally wanted to march off the map before he ended his earthly life. Paul was never satisfied or seduced by his past accomplishments. He kept on pressing on.

Yet, if Paul had allowed it, his past could also have crippled him. Just as he had reason for pride in his heritage, he also had much in his past to be ashamed about too. The apostle could have been paralyzed with guilt. He had held the cloaks of those who had stoned Stephen, the first Christian martyr. He could have cloaked himself with guilt the rest of his life for being an accomplice to that murder and many more. In his religious zeal to commit more murder in the name of religion, he had made it his duty to hunt down Christians. According to the Book of Acts, Paul at that time was like a wild beast stalking and slaughtering the believers. Can you imagine the way he must have felt when he finally became one of those believers himself? Think of it.

Spiritual Atrophy

Not too long ago, a news story told of a forty-year-old man who, because of his overprotective parents, had never been outside the house in which he was born. His parents died, and for four years relatives had brought milk and cheese snacks into the single room in which he lived. Finally someone reported the man's situation to the authorities. When he was taken from the house, they found that his muscles had atrophied. He was so crippled that he couldn't move.

The parallel is easy to see. Paul would testify that there can be a spiritual crippling that can have just as dire consequences over a long period of time. If we give ourselves over to our guilt, punishing ourselves over the years, beating ourselves down, then we will certainly cripple any future effective service. Whatever our mistake—a moment of irresponsibility or immorality or greed committed a month ago, a year ago, a decade ago—if we do not allow the grace of God to cover it and unshackle us from it, we'll certainly become spiritual cripples. And we will never be able to effectively "press on toward the mark of the high calling" of Christian living. Paul was somehow able to do it and we are still benefiting from the results of his effort.

But I can almost hear you saying: "Paul being able to do it is quite a different matter than my being able to do it." Is it really possible for people like us to forget as Paul suggests? Can we control the past instead of letting the past control us?

Good questions. And the answer to both is yes. There is a way to be in control.

The solution lies in understanding this idea of a "holy" amnesia. Consider how Paul did it. In his explanation to the Philippians, he in essence keeps saying over and over, "This one thing I do, this one thing . . . I may be writing epistles and I may be founding churches, but I am really doing one thing. I am straining toward the goal of winning Christ that I might know Him in the fullness of the mystery of all He is."

And Paul went after that priority with characteristic intensity. He says, "I press on . . ." What does that mean? It literally means, I hunt, I chase, I run after this one thing.

How did Paul overcome his past? By the power that focusing on one single priority gave him. Concentration, strangely enough, actually releases power in our lives. Paul didn't suffer from what someone called the "modern psychosis of fragmentation," of thinking that life consists of taking on more and more totally unrelated activities. Anyone who's ever watched what the power of harnessed water can do in making hydroelectric power understands the power of concentration. When we harness that priority and intensity, when we can say that whatever I'm doing I'm doing it for the solitary reason of "winning" Christ as Paul puts it, then we embrace the absolute answer to striving for what lies ahead instead of being a slave to what has been behind.

Such focusing of priority is what kept Paul going, planning, striving—full of energy and life. Not long ago I read a study of Nobel Laureates, those distinguished men and women who have won one of the highest prizes our society offers for achievement. One single trait was noticed in all of them. They didn't stop doing what they were doing because they had won a Nobel prize. In fact, none of them even broke stride. It was characteristic of all of them that they continued pursuing the excellence that haunted them all the previous days of their lives. When Bishop Desmond Tutu was given his Nobel Peace Prize for his work in South Africa, he responded by risking his life as never before in the cause for racial justice. When Carlo Rubbia was given the award for physics, he went straight back to his laboratory and his calculations at Harvard.

When Bruce Merrifield of Rockefeller University received the Nobel prize in chemistry, he simply stepped on the elevator and went back up to the laboratory where he had spent twenty-five years. "It was the worst thing that happened to me," one prize-winner said. "I didn't get any work done the whole year." These great men and women have a sense that what they are doing is more a race than a destination, more a battle than an armistice to be signed. They were focused; they had goals and each strove to reach that goal.

Straining for the Goal

How can any of us live that way? We can, because as Paul put it, we are straining to reach a goal. It was Paul's continuous, persistent goal to strain forward toward that which was ahead. The word comes right out of the athletic world. It refers to a runner whose body is bent over, hands stretched out, head straining forward, eyes riveted on the goal, never daring to look back. How could anyone do that without energy and enthusiasm? That goal is the runner's vital priority. There's nothing casual in this word picture.

In fact, Paul could not imagine a casual commitment to Christ. We can have a casual commitment to an athletic club or a country club or a civic club, but not to our faith. To be focused, to experience that intensity of "pressing on," there can be no casualness in thought or action.

In Colorado Springs there is an institute called The Olympic Athletic Training Center. There they train elite athletes, gathering the thirty greatest track and field athletes in the United States and subjecting them, both men and women, to intense, rigid scrutiny. They are photographed at 2,000 frames a second; their every breath is measured. Coaches even count every heart beat, watch every move the athletes make, searching for the tiniest flaw, hoping to gain one hundredth of a second in a performance time. Here are people who are willing to submit to arduous training to help them reach the mark in the shortest possible time. They will strain for it with all their might.

Why does our society associate that kind of intensity almost exclusively with athletic achievements and goals? Paul went after the Christian life with that kind of intensity, and expected everyone else to do the same. If there is the slightest flaw in my technique, he says, if there is the smallest fault in my pace, I want to correct it, for I've fixed my eye on the goal. I'm living in the now, forgetting the past so that I press on toward the future.

Sometimes it seems that we are saving ourselves for something. But what would it be? Life number two?

Great herds of caribou, 400,000 strong, leave one part of northeastern Canada every year and by instinct make their way across barren land and rushing rivers all the way from Labrador to Hudson Bay to reach their winter grazing grounds. Those people who have seen it say it is one of the awesome spectacles in the natural world. Last year, though, an unusual thing happened. The huge herd of caribou came to one of the great rivers of Canada and found it swollen over its banks. To swim it was to court almost certain death. Instead of turning back or trying a more indirect route, the whole herd plunged straight ahead toward their goal. Over 9,000 didn't make it across. Their bodies were a mute testimony to the inner drive moving the 400,000 toward their goal. They would allow nothing to keep them from reaching the mark.

Paul writes in Philippians that every believer who has encountered the Lord Jesus Christ has been given an indwelling instinct, however we may have muted it. However weak the voice may be from years of neglect, it still calls us upward and onward toward that goal. We *can* forget the past—the good and the bad, so it will not make us stumble. And we *can* focus on that intense priority of the high calling of Christ that keeps us keeping on. There is a holy amnesia and practicing it is one of the healthier ways to keep our souls growing.

🌹 **8** 🌹

Our faith stands on knowing that God does what He will do in His name.

Afterward Moses and Aaron went to Pharaoh and said, "This is what the Lord, the God of Israel, says: 'Let my people go, so that they may hold a festival to me in the desert.'"

Pharaoh said, "Who is the Lord, that I should obey him and let Israel go? I do not know the Lord and I will not let Israel go."

Then they said, "The God of the Hebrews has met with us. Now let us take a three-day journey into the desert to offer sacrifices to the Lord our God, or he may strike us with plagues or with the sword."

But the king of Egypt said, "Moses and Aaron, why are you taking the people away from their labor? Get back to your work!" Then Pharaoh said, "Look, the people of the land are now numerous, and you are stopping them from working."

That same day Pharaoh gave this order to the slave drivers and foremen in charge of the people: "You are no longer to supply the people with straw for making bricks; let them go and gather their own straw. But require them to make the same number of bricks as before; don't reduce the quota. They are lazy; that is why they are crying out, 'Let us go and sacrifice to our God.' Make the work harder for the men so that they keep working and pay no attention to lies . . ."

. . . The Israelite foremen realized they were in trouble . . . they found Moses and Aaron waiting to meet them, and they said, "May the Lord look upon you and judge you! You have made us a stench to Pharaoh and his servants and have put a sword in their hand to kill us."

Moses returned to the Lord and said, "O Lord, why have you brought trouble upon this people? Is this why you sent me? Ever since I went to Pharaoh to speak in your name, he has brought trouble upon this people, and you have not rescued your people at all."

Then the Lord said to Moses, "Now you will see what I will do to Pharaoh. Because of my mighty hand he will let them go . . . I am the Lord. I appeared to Abraham, to Isaac and to Jacob as God Almighty, but by my name the Lord I did not make myself known to them. I also established my covenant with them . . . I have heard the groaning of the Israelites, whom the Egyptians are enslaving, and I have remembered my covenant."

Exodus 5:1–6:5

When Faith Causes
Problems

Dr. Boris Cornfeld was a Jew who lived in Russia during the early years of Communism. Although he was a brilliant, able, informed, and literate young man, he made a mistake. During the great purges of Stalin, he chanced one day to make some kind of political remark. No one knows exactly what he said. Perhaps it was a remark calling into question the absolute wisdom of Stalin or a similar statement. But for some reason, he was immediately arrested and transported to a concentration camp in Siberia.

And there a remarkable thing happened to his life.

Over the months in his cell, he found he was rich in one commodity—time. And he reflected on the roots of his life. He came to see that Marxism—Communism—did not hold the answer to life's deepest needs. He became a prison doctor, and at just that time, God brought across his path a devout Christian who shared gently, quietly, but repeatedly, about Jesus Christ.

At first, it was absolutely out of the question for Boris Cornfeld to turn to Christ. For two hundred years the Russian

Orthodox Church has persecuted his Jewish people, and he could not turn his back on his Jewish heritage and the atrocities of the church.

But his friend persisted, and soon the power of the gospel found a lodging place in his heart. He found himself reciting the Lord's Prayer to the other prisoners as he treated them for medical reasons. Finally, Christ broke through and he quietly but definitely gave his life to Christ, feeling for the first time an overwhelming peace.

But a concentration camp is a dangerous place to live a Christian life. Boris began to live for Christ anyway, in every way, every day. He had watched orderlies steal food from dying prisoner patients, so he began reporting them at the risk of his own life. He began refusing to sign the certificates stating that prisoners were in good enough health to be put in solitary confinement when he knew it would kill them. And he began to share his faith with his patients.

One evening, the doctor was sitting by the bedside of a young man on whom he had performed surgery for cancer of the intestine. As the boy moved in and out of consciousness, the doctor began to share his witness about what Christ had done in his life. The feverish young man would listen to him, as he faded in and out, and Boris stayed by his bed long into the night telling the boy about his faith.

Later that night, the young man heard a commotion in the adjoining room. He found out the next morning that Boris Cornfeld had been clubbed to death by the guards in the concentration camp.

Boris' faith had brought him problems—to the point of death. But the young man to whom he witnessed that night was Aleksandr Solzhenitzyn, the prize-winning Soviet dissident now known the world over. Was Boris' faith worth the problems it caused? Solzhenitzyn would say yes.

But would we? If we were honest, we'd have to admit that when our faith sometimes causes problems in our lives it is altogether confusing. We're not taught that believing will cause problems: we're taught that it solves problems. But it seems that both of these statements are true, to a very real extent.

In fact, there are times, especially for new Christians, that believing has created more problems than it has solved. Even though we may know that faithfulness to God brings long-term dividends—in spite of the fact that it may bring short-term pain—we still find it surprising when our faith causes difficulties in our lives.

The Message of Moses

Moses would confess to that. Fresh from the experience at the burning bush, he went to confront Pharaoh. And there he found rejection not only from Pharaoh but also from the very Hebrew people he was supposed to deliver. Moses, the eighty-year-old, tongue-tied shepherd, found that faithfulness to God brought him expected problems but also unexpected ones. How could he have guessed the people he was to free would turn on him?

Sometimes we know in our hearts that we are doing what God wants us to do. We can just feel the leadership of God in our lives. But then we begin to hit brick wall after brick wall. The pharaohs of this world don't understand. And what may be worse, the very people we're trying to communicate with, to help, aren't accepting us either.

These are the two major causes of problems when we choose to live our Christianity on a daily basis. It was that way for Moses, and it is still that way for us.

Yet, whether we believe it or not, we are promised that when our faithfulness causes problems, God's faithfulness will see us through.

Moses found that to be true—but not before he had experienced his share of frustrating problems. Part of Moses' story in particular tells of God's promise—and helps us understand how to cope, just as Moses did.

Moses and Aaron went to Pharaoh and said, "This is what

the Lord the God of Israel says, 'Let my people go so they may hold a festival to me in the desert.'"

Pharaoh's Response

Pharaoh said, "Who is the Lord that I should obey him and let Israel go? I do not know the Lord and I will not let Israel go."

They tried again, but Pharaoh just shrugged them away. The Pharaoh (probably Ramses II) knew all the gods that counted in his world. In fact, *he* was one of them, according to the way Egyptians believed. He had descended from 3000 years of divine ancestors. His very name meant the "one who is born from the sun god." At that time there were more than eighty major deities in Egypt. Someone once said that if it flew in the air or slithered in the mud or swam through the water, the Egyptians worshiped it.

Ramses told Moses that this god Jehovah hadn't made his list. He knew the sun god and the river god and the frog god but not this Jehovah God. So why should he heed his wishes?

Ironically, within a very short time Pharaoh would be the most informed man in his nation on who Jehovah God is! But at that moment, Pharaoh, supreme ruler in the secular world, didn't even recognize the God Moses represented and neither was he impressed by His people.

Pharaoh would have measured the Hebrew people's God by how successful the people were. It only made sense. That was the way of the ancient world. And so, the Egyptians thought, since they were the most powerful nation on earth, their gods obviously were the most powerful. If the God of these Hebrew slaves wanted to impress Ramses, He'd have to do better with this nation of slaves.

But there's nothing unusual about that, is there? The same is true today. Yet God always seems to choose the foolish things of this world for His work to shame the wise, as Paul puts it in 1 Corinthians.

I've been reading a certain major news magazine weekly for over twenty years, ever since college. I read it almost cover to cover. And I've noticed that every time there is a story about evangelicals, the tone is quite condescending. According to the way most of these news stories portray us, you'd think we were all mindless religious fanatics unworthy of consideration. That tone used to bother me quite a bit.

But now I understand the situation and it doesn't bother me as it once did. That magazine is a thoroughly secular and humanistic publication. If it ever started to compliment evangelicals something would be very wrong!

You see, the fact of the matter is that the secular world, the unbelieving world, does not recognize God or the people who serve as His body. In fact, secularists are usually quite surprised at our audacity, our way of looking at everything in this world quite differently.

Ramses was dumbfounded by Moses' audacity. Ramses' mission in life, it seemed, was to build bigger and bigger statues, mainly of himself. He was one of the greatest builders in history. The British Museum in London holds just one of the gigantic statues of himself he built. Ramses had to have bricks; he also had to have slave labor to make as many statues as cheaply and as quickly as possible. How dare this scruffy Moses ask for his slaves to stop making the bricks for his important work just so they could go make some burnt offerings and have a feast in the desert? Didn't this Moses understand what was really important?

The same goes for people involved in a purely secular lifestyle. It must seem audacious for us to interrupt them in their day-to-day living to remind them that God wants a word with them. They need to know there is something out there more important than building bigger and better statues to themselves!

I remember being with a group of people who were witnessing door-to-door in a suburb of our city. We ran into a fellow whose reaction to us wasn't so much anger as amazement. "Why do you people go around doing this?" he asked. How could we answer in any way that he would understand? His frame of reference was totally different from ours so there was no way he could view our efforts as anything but unusual.

We Christians face rejection from the secular world because, just as in Pharaoh Ramses' day, the world does not understand the agenda of faith. God's agenda was worship. Pharaoh's was to get on with the business of building. Surely these people were using their so-called religion to get out of work, Ramses must have thought. This religion of theirs is nothing but irresponsibility. It's childish and lazy. He knew what really counted. And that's the way it is with many of the people in our world. I remember one man in particular who looked me in the face and said, "Why would a man like you waste your time as a minister when you could be doing something productive with your life?"

The day I stopped being thunderstruck at the world's lack of understanding was the day I began to understand the tension between a faith that causes problems and a faith that resolves them. There is a peace that comes with understanding that we're on a different agenda than the secular-minded world. We cannot expect them to understand us, but we *can* understand *them*.

The People's Reaction

Yet, what do we do when, like Moses, the difficulties come not from the thoroughly secular world, but from the people we are trying to help—even from those who claim to believe as we do?

Moses found out that it was one thing to be rejected by Pharaoh, but it was quite another to be rejected by the very people whom God had sent him to serve. I wouldn't have blamed Moses for thinking he was one for three in the success department. He struck out as a baby when he was sent down the river in a basket. He struck out again at forty when he tried to do the right thing the wrong way—attempting to help his people yet killing an Egyptian. And now, here he was at eighty, coming back for the third time feeling as if he were going to strike out again.

Do you remember what happened? All Moses' effort caused Pharaoh to proclaim that the lazy Hebrew people would not only have to make just as many bricks as before—but without any straw! They would have to go out and work doubly hard obtaining the raw materials themselves for the bricks. The Hebrew foreman walked up to Moses and Aaron and said, "May the Lord look upon you and judge you. You have made us a stench to Pharaoh and his servants, and you have put a sword in their hands to kill us."

"Why did you even get involved with this?" the foreman was asking Moses. It seemed he had only made things worse. Surely, Moses was upset. He must have thought that at least the Hebrews wanted an exodus before he got involved. Now it appeared they didn't want anything. The people he was trying to help, who seemed at first to want his help, now were cursing him for making things worse.

Many of us know the feeling. How can things get worse before they get better when we do things in the name of our faith? It's part of the Christian experience more often than not. We get involved, we give ourselves, we take a stand with people or for people, and just because we're being obedient to God, everything begins to crumble.

I remember the first time it happened to me. It was my first pastorate in a tiny little church in a poor part of Waco, Texas. There was a woman who had moved from the north into a big, ramshackle house on one of the streets in our neighborhood. She needed every kind of help in the book: food, clothing, and money to get the house's utilities turned on. And on top of everything else she had a sick baby. It seemed I poured my life into ministering to her. I took food to her, transported her baby to the county clinic (sitting with her for hours there), and then I arranged for her utilities to be turned on. I did all the things I thought I was supposed to do. And yet, when I went by there on the next Sunday morning to ask her to come to our church, she nearly pushed me off her porch, saying, "I never want to see you again!"

What's going on, Lord? I remember wondering. *I got involved to help and now I've been misunderstood and rejected.*

When faithfulness brings problems we may quickly find that our only resource is in a renewed cry of prayer to the living God. That's what Moses did. He went back to square one. He went back to God, saying in essence, "Lord, why have You brought trouble upon Your people? Is this why You sent me? Ever since I went to Pharaoh to speak in Your name, he has caused trouble for me and for them—and You haven't rescued either of us. Why did You get me involved in this? Why is all this happening?"

It's almost as if Moses was reminding God what they had talked about at the burning bush—how Moses had given God some very good excuses why the whole idea wouldn't work.

And then God gave him the answer. God told Moses that He was waiting for Moses, and everyone around him, to run out of every other resource other than the living God. "Now you will see what I will do to Pharaoh," He explained to Moses. "Because of My mighty hand, he will let them go. And because of My mighty hand he will drive them out after he himself has cried out to Me."

It's as if God was telling Moses that He was waiting until everyone found out that Pharaoh is not the resource—God was. Some of the Hebrews at the time thought they were going to pull off the exodus by "committee."

The Israelite foremen had gone and appealed to Pharaoh (and the word "appeal" here is the very word that is usually translated in the Old Testament as "prayer to God"). The "committee" of Hebrews at this point felt God was unpredictable and capricious, while Pharaoh was predictable and steadfast. But through all of this, they began to realize that it was actually the opposite. Pharaoh was the fickle one, while God was steadfast. If there was to be an exodus, they were going to have to trust the Lord Jehovah.

We're in the Picture, Too

Don't we see this truth in our own experience? How many times have we had to reach the end of our own resources before we remembered to trust in God, the one steadfast resource of our lives? We're all in need of a spiritual exodus day by day. When our faith causes difficulties, our first response is to fall back on our familiar resources—people, things, self—and only when these do not help can we truly lean only upon God for our needs.

I like what Dwight L. Moody said about Moses in this connection. Moody, not a very erudite man, had an unusual insight into the scripture. He said that Moses spent forty years in the king's palace thinking that he was somebody; then he lived forty years in the wilderness finding out that without God he was a nobody; finally he spent forty more years discovering how a nobody with God can be a somebody.

And he was right. When Moses and the people found out they were nobodies without the resource of God, that's when the exodus began.

But beyond this recognition, there is more we will receive when our faithfulness brings problems. We will receive renewed personal assurance. God promised faithfulness to Moses based on nothing but God's faithfulness to His own name. Over and over, when God explained to Moses what to say and do, He told Moses to say, "I am the Lord," to remind the people that his power and trustworthiness were based on His own name alone. ". . . Then you will know that I am the Lord." Over and over, Jehovah uses the phrase in conversation with Moses. If you remember, up to this time, the name of God had been called into question. Pharaoh had taken God's name lightly, daring to ask, "Who is this Jehovah?" And so God stated that He would do all He was going to do because "I am the Lord."

There won't be an exodus because Pharaoh's heart changed. His heart will never change. There won't be an exodus because the Hebrews stopped being fickle. They will always be fickle. There won't be an exodus because Moses is a brave, courageous leader. Moses will stammer all his life. There will be an exodus for only one reason, and that is: "I am the Lord."

The biggest promise we have as we live this life of faith is not that the Pharaohs of our secular world will change, or that the people we try to help will change. The only reason we are assured any victory at all over these problems is not that God's people are suddenly constant and never fickle, but because God is faithful to His own name. God's name in Christ is written all over us. And the same faith that resolves our problems will be the faith that is victorious over the problems—because we are God's in God's name.

Suppose I tell my little boy that we are going to take a walk after dinner and we'll have a good time—then I don't do it. The world will not stop. But a little boy's world will be different because the one he calls father, "Daddy," would be remembered for something said and yet not done. Yet our faith stands on knowing that God does what He says He will do in His name. Jesus, from the cross, cried, "My God, My God! Why hast Thou forsaken Me?" Those words hung heavy over the borrowed tomb where they laid Jesus' dead body. And yet on that third day, out of faithfulness to His very name, Christ was resurrected, forsaken no more. Our hope is built on that faithfulness.

Our own weaknesses will ebb and flow. But God has declared He will be faithful to His own name and those who live and act under that Name. So, when all other resources fail, when our Christian gestures seem to cause nothing but problems from our secular surroundings, from those we try to help, or even from our fellow Christians, the one thing we must keep in mind is that our faith is constant and timeless because our truest Resource is everlasting and persevering.

Our personal assurance is clear: If we endure, our faithfulness *will* be rewarded and the results will be worth the difficulties.

🌹 9 🌹

After we have experienced the grace and forgiveness of the Lord
Jesus Christ, we must then live it by forgiving one another.

Then Peter came to Jesus and asked, "Lord, how many times shall I forgive my brother when he sins against me? Up to seven times?"

Jesus answered, "I tell you, not seven times, but seventy-seven times.

"Therefore, the kingdom of heaven is like a king who wanted to settle accounts with his servants. As he began the settlement, a man who owed him ten thousand talents was brought to him. Since he was not able to pay, the master ordered that he and his wife and his children and all that he had be sold to repay the debt.

"The servant fell on his knees before him. 'Be patient with me,' he begged, 'and I will pay back everything.' The servant's master took pity on him, canceled the debt and let him go.

"But when that servant went out, he found one of his fellow servants who owed him a hundred denarii. He grabbed him and began to choke him. 'Pay back what you owe me!' he demanded.

"His fellow servant fell to his knees and begged him, 'Be patient with me, and I will pay you back.'

"But he refused. Instead, he went off and had the man thrown into prison until he could pay the debt. When the other servants saw what had happened, they were greatly distressed and went and told their master everything that had happened.

"Then the master called the servant in. 'You wicked servant,' he said, 'I canceled all that debt of yours because you begged me to. Shouldn't you have had mercy on your fellow servant just as I had on you? In anger his master turned him over to the jailers until he should pay back all he owed.

"This is how my heavenly Father will treat each of you unless you forgive your brother from your heart."

Matthew 18:21-35

Forgiveness —
Disgracing Grace

Simon Isenthall, a famous Jewish writer, wrote a remarkable short story in 1976 entitled "The Sunflower." It was an autobiographical account of an experience he'd had thirty years before while incarcerated in a German concentration camp. While on a work detail turning a barn into a field hospital, he was stopped by a young German nurse who said, "Come quickly, come quickly." She guided him to a young man whose head was wrapped with a blood-soaked bandage covering both eyes. Grabbing for Isenthall's hand, the young man finally caught it with a death grip and cried out, "I must talk to a Jew before I die!"

Isenthall said, "I am a Jew."

The young man said, "My SS troop was sent to burn down a Jewish house. After it was set on fire, the family ran out of the house, and we gunned them down. I cannot get it out of my mind. I know I am about to die. Forgive me!"

Isenthall said in "The Sunflower":

"I jerked my hand away and went out the door without a word . . . That bothered me for thirty years." And then he ended the story in a most unusual way. He told of asking thirty-two different people to comment on his reaction. They were Jews, Gentiles, young and old, men and women. Out of the thirty-two people polled, the majority said that he did the right thing, that he should not have forgiven. One of them said that the young soldier should go straight to hell.

The late Corrie ten Boom found herself in a similar situation. During the war she and her sister were also imprisoned in a concentration camp. They were taken continually to the delousing shower and forced to strip naked. A lecherous SS guard ogled these very modest women during the whole humiliating time. Corrie survived the camp, but her sister did not.

After the war, Corrie became a Christian spokeswoman all over the world, preaching forgiveness everywhere she went. One day she was speaking in Munich. At the end of the lecture, a man came up to her and stuck out his hand and said, "Ah yes, God's forgiveness is good, isn't it?" As she looked into his face, she recognized him as the lecherous SS guard. His face had been imprinted on her consciousness forever. She said, "I thought in my heart I had forgiven him, [but] as he reached his hand out, my hand froze by my side, and I could not reach out and take his hand. Here I was, the world-famous forgiver, and I had come face to face with a man I couldn't even touch. I prayed to God, 'God, forgive me for my inability to forgive.' When I asked God for that, He gave me the grace to reach my hand out, take that man's hand, and say, 'Yes, God is good.'"

Something similar must have happened to or among the disciples during those years of following Jesus across the Holy Land. Maybe it was Peter, or maybe it was Andrew or John, but obviously, as the story is told in Matthew 18, somebody needed to forgive someone else. Peter came to Jesus and asked, "Lord, how many times shall I forgive my brother when he sins against me, up to seven times?" The rabbis of the time always taught that a person should forgive another person three times. So Peter, feeling magnanimous, doubled that and added one for good measure. And Jesus answered, "I tell you not seven times, but seventy-seven," which was His way of pointing out to Peter that he had fallen far short of Jesus' conception of forgiveness. It was as if Jesus were saying, "As long as you are talking about limitations on forgiveness, you've not understood the message of the kingdom of God that I've come to bring."

We all know how it feels to be deeply hurt. People can betray our confidence or our trust, crush our feelings, or even harm us physically. How can anyone who has been wronged by another human being possibly be so forgiving as to *keep* on forgiving?

A Story of Forgiveness

I'm sure Jesus understood the sheer incredulity that the disciples must have displayed after His answer. And so He told a parable to explain such forgiveness. It was one of His most unusual stories, a drama in several acts. Even the setting of the parable was strange. The setting, scholars tell us, is not that of the Holy Land, but of some kingdom much further to the East, perhaps in what we would today call Iran or Iraq.

In this land, as Jesus told the story, a king suddenly wants to know what he is worth. These were the days long before modern-day accounting or bookkeeping—not to mention personal computers. The only way a king could find out what he was worth was to have his servants come in and put all he owned, and all that was owed him, on the table and count it. And that's exactly what the king did.

Jesus explained, "The kingdom of heaven is like the king who wanted to settle accounts with his servants." The king ran his fingers over the list of debts owed to him by his servants and decided he wanted everyone to pay up. At that time servants were not houseboys waving fans to keep flies off the king. Servants were men of enormous responsibility. Today we might call them cabinet-level members of the government, vice-regents of the kingdom.

The first one to enter the presence of the king was a man who owed him 10,000 talents. This man had defrauded the king. It's difficult to estimate what 10,000 talents means. To give you a comparison, all the taxes collected by Herod the Great when he was king of Israel amounted to only around 800 talents a year. All of the gold in the Ark of the Covenant was only 30 talents. Ten thousand talents was probably the amount of money that was in the biggest bank in the Eastern Roman Empire—the bank on the Acropolis of Athens. We would say today that this man had done the equivalent of robbing Fort Knox—right under his master's nose. He owed him something between 30 and 50 million dollars (since a day's wages was 17¢, this would look like our modern national debt!).

How would the king respond? In the modern Arab world officials cut off a man's hands if he is caught in simple theft. In that day, this servant must have thought that his head was forfeit. For some reason, Jesus tells us that since the servant was not able to pay, the king ordered that the servant, his wife, his children, and all that he had be sold to pay the debt. Possibly, Jesus included this point in the story to show the absolutely impossible situation of this servant. Because even if the servant's assets were totally liquidated, it would not have equaled even one ten thousandth of what he owed the king. With the going rate of slaves at the time, the man's whole family would not have brought one gold talent. Because of this hopeless condition, he sorely needed mercy, grace, and forgiveness.

As you might imagine, and as we all probably would have done, the servant gasped out a seemingly futile appeal. He fell on his knees and begged, "Be patient with me and I will pay back everything." He knew his situation was hopeless, so he tried everything he could do, falling on his knees, pleading for "patience." The word in the Greek New Testament combines the word for "long" with the word "temper" and means literally to be "long-tempered." We have the opposite English word, "short-tempered," so we can understand the idea. It means to postpone any action or retaliation.

There was a problem with his plea, though, wasn't there? He discounted it with an impossible lie. He said, "I will pay back everything." At the daily wage of the time, it would have taken him one hundred million years to do that! He didn't even have 60 million *minutes* left to live if he was in midlife.

So, such a lie would make the king angrier, you'd think. But as it happens in Jesus' unpredictable parables, the punch line is quite surprising. The king took pity on this man, canceled the debt, and let him go. Moved only by pity, since this man had done nothing to deserve such forgiveness, the king wiped his slate clean.

One scholar stated in discussing this story, "In that civilization, such an act would never have been done without also giving him back his full responsibility and trusting him to be a steward once again."

Where Do We Fit In?

If we hold this story up to a mirror, we will understand that it is a story most of all about the sovereignty of God. Everyone of us has been given the stuff of life—one or more talents. Time, money, energy, connections, influence, contacts, life itself—all are gifts. It is a story of every person, because we've all fallen short of what God intended for us when He gave us our bundle of talents. Sometimes, He even catches us red-handed—and we feel it when the Holy Spirit convicts us. At such times, we feel our own mortality, even to the extent of saying such things as, "Just give me time and I'll pay it back." Down deep we know our pleas are just as futile as the servant's.

The difficulty with sin, the breaking of God's law, is that it doesn't just place us in a difficult situation. It places us in an *impossible* situation apart from the mercy of God. And there is no way to take back the resulting effects of the sin. Like throwing a pebble into a still country pond, the concentric circles of responsibility, of problems, only spread wider and wider. There's no going back, no repayment of even a moment of our disobedience.

Of course, it's easy to see the personal correlation in this part of the parable. It's as if Jesus is standing up and saying, "I've already paid your debt on the cross." Like the father of the prodigal He comes and says, "Welcome back." Like a king coming down from his throne He says, "You're a commoner, but I'll make you royalty." Like a judge stepping down from the bench and becoming the defense attorney, He says, "You're mine. I forgive you fully, freely, finally, forever."

It's hard to understand what a relief such forgiveness can bring if you yourself haven't been forgiven a huge debt. I remember the first time that happened to me. I was nineteen years old, and pastoring a church in south Waco, just off the Baylor University campus. The community surrounding the church was a slum. I was ministering to one of the most desperate groups of people I had ever met. But I was happy to be there, and I was ready to win everybody to Christ. I had lots of enthusiasm, but very little knowledge.

In that church there was a young man whose wife was expecting a baby. So, when the time came, I went with them to the hospital and sat there all day long—twelve hours. All the time I was thinking, *If I just sit here with him long enough, I'll surely win him to the Lord.* While we were there, I went with him to the hospital business office. There they shoved a piece of paper toward him and asked him to fill it out. I discovered that he couldn't write. He didn't even have a job, and he couldn't pay the debt. So in my wonderful pastoral wisdom, I said, "Oh, give it to me. I'll sign it." I was sure the man would get a job the next week and he'd always remember how I'd helped him with his problem.

He didn't get a job, and within the month my new bride and I had received the hospital bill. To make everything even worse, I found out that there was another baby already on the account from the year before. I had signed to pay for *two* deliveries! At that moment, I, a college freshman, saw my whole life passing before my eyes. I thought I had ruined my reputation and my good name forever.

In desperation, I visited the administrator of the hospital (he happened to be a deacon in a large church in the city). I told him I was just a young preacher. He said, "Yes, I can see that, all right." I admitted I had done a very foolish thing. He said, "Yes, we know what you did. And we've already taken care of it. We have an account for such things."

I almost went through the roof of that hospital I was so happy. It was as if I had thrown off an impossibly heavy weight. I owed a debt I couldn't pay. And it had been paid for me.

Why do I tell you all this? The servant should have felt as I did when my debt was wiped away. All this is only the background for the point that the parable makes. It is actually the backdrop for the central act of this drama.

When the servant left the king, he did not act the way you would have expected him to respond in the face of his forgiveness. He should have had a new lease on life. He should have felt reborn. Instead, he did something unbelievable. He went out to disgrace the grace he had been given.

Jesus explained that the servant "went out and found one of his fellow servants." There's an emphasis on that word "found." It doesn't mean that one of his fellow servants crossed his path. It means that he deliberately went out to find him. The fellow servant owed the forgiven servant 100 denarii, or about $17 in today's currency. That would come to about 100 days' wages, a sum most men could have handled, given enough time. Suddenly the man with the huge debt was now a stern creditor. We are told he grabbed his fellow servant and began choking him, saying, "Pay me back what you owe me!"

Livy, the Roman historian, tells us that according to Roman law if a man owed you money you could twist his neck until the blood ran from his nostrils. Evidently, the forgiven servant was doing just that.

It's interesting to contrast the two scenes. Only a moment before, this man had been treated with dignity. Now he is humiliating another man whose debt is trivial compared to his own. And then his own words are thrown back to him when the fellow servant says, "Be patient with me and I will pay you back." Yet the forgiven servant acts as if he does not recognize those words. In this case, the possibility of the debt being repaid was very real. It may have taken several months, but it was possible.

Yet you can almost hear the spring door slam shut on the forgiven servant's hard heart. He actually has his fellow servant thrown into prison until he can pay this small debt. In reality, he ruined the man's life forever. Debtor's prison was a futile institution, since you couldn't work to pay the debt until you could get out—and you couldn't get out until you had paid the debt. He killed hope in that man's life forever.

The Point of It All

What is the point in this story? I believe that Jesus is teaching a lesson in memory. He knows that we will be slighted, offended, betrayed, even hurt in this lifetime by other human beings. And He knows that we must react. But he wants us to remember something before we react.

After we have experienced the grace and forgiveness of the Lord Jesus Christ, we must then live it by forgiving one another. Why? Because comparing what others have done to you with the enormity of what God has forgiven you in His grace is like comparing the Pacific Ocean with a mud puddle. It is like comparing Mount Everest with a molehill. There is no comparison. Seventy times seven, indeed!

Martin Luther, the great reformer, put it this way. "When you have experienced Christ, you must go out to be like Christ toward others."

There is a certain tribe of Polynesians who keep the shrunken heads of their enemies hanging in the doorways of their huts. The purpose of this strange action is to remind one another from generation to generation to remain angry at their enemies.

Some of us hang things in our hearts just like that. They are tokens of bitterness to remind us to stay angry and unforgiving toward someone else.

Yet forgiveness is a foundation for the vital Christian life. Forgiveness isn't a concept to be left in a theological fog. At one time or another, it must be grappled with by all of us.

In his book *Forgive and Forget* (Harper and Row, 1984) Lewis Smedes says some very basic things about forgiveness. He states that when it comes to forgiving because you have been forgiven, there are three stages you must go through: recognition, surgery, and starting over.

Recognition

First, you must recognize that something has happened to you that really deserves forgiveness. This factor can be misunderstood. Hurt may lead to forgiveness, but not every hurt is serious enough to require forgiveness. Sometimes we cheapen forgiveness by forgiving things that really don't rise to the level of needing forgiveness.

Have you ever had the experience of someone coming to ask you to forgive them for something you didn't even know they had done? There are some minor matters that you ought to have the grace and grits just to forget. They don't even rise to the level of requiring forgiveness.

What do I mean? For instance, someone cuts in front of you in line at the grocery store, someone is late for an appointment, a colleague is rude to you at a party, a friend doesn't notice you, the boss didn't invite you to his daughter's wedding. You don't have to forgive such people. You just accept the grace of God to go on, to not allow life's slights and oversights to entangle you. When you become bitter about things that don't even deserve your time, then you cheapen forgiveness.

What then needs forgiving? Two things—betrayal and disloyalty. These are the two wounds that need to be recognized and confronted.

Examples? A husband, after fifteen years of marriage, is unfaithful to his wife; a business partner who promises a friend a loan and then reneges because he can make more money by loaning it to another; a co-worker who recommends a friend to the boss for promotion until he finds the friend is out of favor with the boss and hurriedly withdraws the recommendation. That is disloyalty which deserves confronting and forgiving. And then there is betrayal: A person shares the deepest secrets of his/her life with someone in confidence and that person tells it to the neighborhood's biggest gossip. Disloyalty and betrayal are the two experiences worthy of forgiveness, worthy of recognition.

Surgery

Then, after recognizing these situations, there needs to be surgery. In other words, you simply cut away from the person the disloyalty or betrayal that they have done to you. You disengage the person from the act. Actually, when you get right down to what forgiveness is, it is this very step, done through the grace of God.

Starting Over

Then the third stage of forgiveness is starting over. Picture a father going to a daughter whom he has disowned and saying, "I want you to be my daughter again." Or picture one friend going to another after a tremendous falling-out and saying, "I want you to be my friend again. I want to start over again."

That sounds like the hardest thing in the world to do, when you apply it to a personal situation, doesn't it? But is it any harder to wake up every morning with that same unforgiving spirit, that same bitterness beating you over the head? Is it any harder than running the same tape through your mind over and over, day after day, month after month, year after year of hatred, vengeance, and anger because you won't forgive? Maybe the hardest part of the whole situation is bearing and living with the slow decay such lack of forgiveness forces upon your soul.

That's why Jesus tells this parable, to show it is an act of grace to clear up the situation and clear it out of your life.

The parable has a sober final act. Fellow servants saw the whole incident between the forgiven man and his fellow servant. Someone is always watching what we do. If these servants had truly been merciful, they would have paid the fellow servant's debt. Instead they ran and told the king what they saw: "You know that man you forgave 10,000 golden talents? You aren't going to believe what he just did over 100 denarii!"

For the first time in the story, the king is angry. When he was betrayed, he wasn't angry. But when he found that the one he had forgiven fully had himself refused to forgive, then he became very angry indeed.

What follows is the "divine must," the moral of the story. "Shouldn't you have mercy on your fellow servant just as I had mercy on you?" the king, in essence, asks. The "should" is actually a "must," and is the same word in the Greek New Testament that

Jesus uses when He said three times, "The Son of Man must go to the cross." It's that divine imperative which is part of the whole salvation experience. If we know grace, we must forgive. We must want to forgive.

A nurse who called herself Sue wrote in *Guideposts* about a true experience she had. She was at her nurse's station on a bleak and snowy January evening late at night when she decided to check on room 712. The man had suffered a light heart attack and everything seemed to be just fine. His vital signs were okay.

But as she was about to leave, he grabbed the sheets until his knuckles turned white, pulled himself up, and said, "Please call my daughter." Sue tried to calm him down, but he said, "No, you don't understand, she's the only child I have. Please call her now." Sue noticed his breathing had become ragged and labored. She adjusted the oxygen and left to call his daughter, when he suddenly called after her, "Do you have any paper, nurse?" She had one little yellow scrap of paper in her pocket and so she handed it to him.

When she called the daughter, she knew the daughter would be upset to know about her father's heart attack but she wasn't prepared for her reaction. "Oh no!" the daughter sobbed. "Please, no! Tell me that he'll get better!" It sounded more like a plea than a request for information. "You don't understand," the daughter cried. "A year ago, we had a terrible argument and the last time I saw my father, I slammed the door and went out screaming, 'I hate you!'"

Not too long after she hung up the phone, Sue decided to check on the man in room 712 again. She noticed he was all too still, checked his pulse and found none, and began CPR while waiting for the emergency team to arrive. But the team was too late. One by one, the team left the room until finally someone turned off the gurgling oxygen machine. And then all was absolutely quiet. Nurse Sue was the last one to leave the room. And there she noticed a doctor in conversation with a young woman who had to be the man's daughter.

As she walked into her father's room, the daughter began to sob. Convulsively, she grabbed the sheet over her father and pulled it up to her eyes sobbing even more uncontrollably. Just as she did, the nurse looked over and saw the yellow piece of paper she had handed the man. On the paper, he had written, "I love you. I forgive you. I hope that you forgive me. I know you don't hate me." Signed, "Daddy."

Isn't it sad that only one half of the relationship was put right? The daughter, though given the cleansing of her father's wonderful forgiveness, did not have the chance to make it reciprocal as she wanted so desperately to do at that sad, irreversible moment.

Forgiving is so treacherously hard. But when we cannot forgive, we are actually disgracing the grace we already have experienced.

How can we forgive? Remembering all we've been forgiven, and remembering Who has done that forgiving is the secret to making that first move into active, life-affirming forgiveness, no matter what the hurt.

❦ 10 ❦

Faith is its own reward. We cannot expect a rose garden bonus for believing. In reality, we will know many of the same problems as non-Christians and maybe some that non-Christians will never know.

To keep me from becoming conceited because of these sur-passingly great revelations, there was given me a thorn in my flesh, a messenger of Satan, to torment me.

Three times I pleaded with the Lord to take it away from me. But he said to me, "My grace is sufficient for you, for my power is made perfect in weakness."

Therefore I will boast all the more gladly about my weak-nesses, so that Christ's power may rest on me. That is why, for Christ's sake, I delight in weaknesses, in insults, in hardships, in persecutions, in difficulties. For when I am weak, then I am strong.

2 Corinthians 12:7–10

Crisis—
Why Me?

A fine Christian woman found herself suddenly in the hospital. The doctors had discovered that she had a very serious case of cancer. An active member of her church, she soon found herself deluged with visitors. And with those visitors, she also found herself deluged with quite a myriad of different theories on why she was going through this crisis and how to cope with the crisis as a Christian.

The people who came to visit were good, well-intentioned people, just like you and I. But, she remembered five distinct categories. One was the well-meaning deacon who told her that there was a reason she was sick. Either she must have done something displeasing in her life, or at the very least there must be something that God wanted to teach her through it.

The second was a somewhat scatterbrained lady who swooped in bringing flowers and singing hymns. She was sort of a cheerleader for the sick. As they visited, every time the cancer victim brought up her illness, the woman would not let her talk. The woman simply voiced one platitude after another and then breezed out.

The third visitor was a woman who told her that healing was the answer. The visitor's message was that God doesn't want anybody to be sick—ever—and that her only hope was for God to heal her. And then the visitor said that God would definitely do just that if the woman's faith was strong enough.

Later that day, the woman remembered this visitor's words while she was lying on a cold table undergoing a cobalt treatment. So she concentrated, trying to muster up a stronger faith. But her mind stopped. Something about the situation caused her to realize what she was doing was wrong. Faith isn't like a muscle—more supple and resilient when exercised, she realized. It's just *there*.

Then the most "spiritual" person in her congregation visited her. "If you'll praise God in everything, *everything*, you'll soon be able to thank God for what has happened to you!" the man said. Suddenly, she had this grotesque image of God pop into her head: He wasn't a heavenly Father, but a gigantic troll, a monster, holding her by one foot, and squeezing her until she finally gasped, "Thank You!" She grimaced at the thought, closing her eyes in exasperation.

Finally, the pastor entered her room. He told her that God had chosen her to share in the suffering of Christ, in the koinonia of His fellowship because He knew in His infinite wisdom that she could bear this with integrity and be a blessing to others. After he left, though, she wondered, *If that's so, why did He pick me? There are millions of Christians stronger than I am. Couldn't He have found someone else to be a better example?*

Job's False Friend

This woman's well-wishers remind me of Job's friends. As soon as they heard about Job's troubles, they came to him. They found him sitting in the ashes, having lost everything. And what did they do? They began spouting reasons about why it all had happened. Job's friends, it seems, came not so much to comfort Job as to uncover some logical reason for his troubles.

And so do we. We can't stand the idea of not knowing *why*. And so we give advice, speculate, and worry. We even cajole God to explain the universe to us.

Why do bad things happen to us? Philosophers have tried to discover the answer to that question for centuries. There are scores of ponderous volumes concerning that one question. But we still don't know the answer, and it would be presumptuous to say we did.

Yet, we must consider it. Sometimes such crises are avenues for amazing spurts of growth. But sometimes they are "faith-busters."

What's the difference?

The difference seems to lie in the person—how he or she responds. Not how he or she understands.

We all know about Paul's "thorn" in the flesh, as it is called. But "thorn" may not be a strong enough word. The Greek word used here means a "stake," a great "nail," more often than it does a tiny thorn. In fact, the word was sometimes used to mean "impaled," to run someone through. It could mean the cross itself.

But Paul tells us he was "given" this thorn, this spike through his flesh. It could even be translated, "for" his flesh. And we are left to wonder what that thorn was. Some have said it was a form of malaria; others say it was some kind of hysteria or painful eye disease. And some people believe strongly that Paul had epileptic seizures. Whatever it was, we know from Paul's words that it was painful enough for him to call it a "stake" in his flesh.

What sort of cue can we take from Paul about how to respond to our own great thorns?

It's Okay to Ask Why?

First, we don't have to feel guilty about questioning, about asking God for a reason for our crisis. Very "spiritual" types may give you the idea that it is wrong to wonder why things are happening. But often, asking such a question will be the beginning of a way through, if not a way out—even if answers aren't forthcoming. So, it's okay to ask. That's what Paul did.

Twice in this letter he says that God allowed him to have this "thorn" to keep him from becoming conceited from "great revelations." Evidently, from the first verses of this chapter, we can read that Paul had been given these supernatural, uplifting visions. Then, when he asked God why he had such pain, God said, "Paul, to keep you from being conceited." And then he repeats it, in case we missed it.

There are several kinds of pride. There is the pride of "face," the pride of "race," and the pride of "grace." Some of us don't have much to be proud of when it comes to the pride of "face," but quite a number of us have a kind of insidious pride of "race," feeling we are better than others.

But I believe the worst form of pride is the pride of "grace," being proud about the spiritual grace that has come into our lives— through no act of our own. And that could easily have been Paul's temptation. He needed to keep himself from conceit, from arrogance, from spiritual pride.

Paul, then, was beginning to see reasons for his crisis. But we know all too well that God doesn't normally give reasons. Most of the time He doesn't. And it can drive us crazy.

A friend of mine, a professor at a Christian college, is a wonderful Christian lady. One day a car ran a red light, plowed into her car, and almost killed her. As she rested in the hospital, coping with the pain from her awful injuries, she said that she had a whole series of visitors and everyone of them wanted to speculate about the reason why God had permitted this to happen to her.

She told me, "As I went in and out of consciousness, I simply wanted to be conscious of resting in the arms of Jesus whom I knew loved me. But all these people wanted to talk about was why would God allow this to happen to such a 'good lady' as I was. I felt so bad that I wasn't the least bit interested."

When we begin to try to put reasons into God's mouth for what happens to us, they always sound forced. I think of one young man who, when his father suddenly died, had to fit it into the grand scheme of God's design. So finally, he said, "Well, I know why God did it. With Dad's social security money, I'll be able to go to college." He hadn't given a thought to why his mother was left a widow and why his three younger brothers and sisters were deprived of a father. He wanted his suffering to make sense so bad that his efforts sounded shrill and hollow. And futile.

That's usually the way it is when we grope around for answers. The only answers that won't sound hollow or narrow are the ones from God, and yet God doesn't usually give reasons as He did to Paul. Instead, what He offers is Himself.

God Spoke to Job

Look at the story of Job. That amazing book is not so much about Job's suffering as it is a book about the overwhelming presence of God. At the end of the book, after the bad advice of Job's friends, and after Job's own questions, God finally speaks. It is the longest speech that God makes in the entire Bible. Yet God doesn't give Job a single answer to any of the questions Job raised.

Speaking out of a storm, God says instead, "Who is this that darkens my counsel with words without knowledge? Brace yourself like a man. I will question you and you will answer Me." And then He asks, "Where were you when I laid the earth's foundation?" For four chapters, as Frederick Buechner puts it, God does not explain, God explodes. And at the end of it all, Job is left reeling. I would imagine it almost knocked him flat. God didn't give him information. Instead, He gave Job revelation—of Who He was, and is.

And how did Job respond? That answer was enough to make Job fall down and worship God. In chapter 42 Job says, "I know that you can do all things. No plan of yours can be thwarted . . . . Surely I spoke of things that I did not understand, things too wonderful for me to know." The picture seems to be of a gracious and loving covenant between God and Job, as if God told him, in words we can relate to: "Job, you can no more understand my grand design than I could explain Einstein's theories to a clam." Job was humbled, and he worshiped.

God Spoke to Paul

Most often, then, God does not give reasons as He did for Paul, but He gives Himself as He did for Job. Maybe that is better in the long run. Why? We would do just as Paul did. We'd ask for God to remove this bad thing.

Three times Paul pleads with God to take his thorn away. There is a feeling of utter pathos in his words. Paul was an old, broken man. He knew what it was like to be stoned and left for dead, to be beaten, to float in the wreckage of a sunken ship in the Mediterranean. And yet, Paul begged God to take this hurt away. I would imagine Paul even went to his friend Dr. Luke and asked if there was anything he could do. Obviously, though, nothing could be done. And nothing was done.

Did Paul, one of the Bible's spiritual giants, have problems with the fact God would not do as he asked Him to?

I'm sure he did. The eighteenth-century agnostic philosopher David Hume summarized the problem of why God doesn't remove problems from people's lives. Hume said, in effect, "If God is able to take the hurt away, but is not willing, He is a malevolent, evil God. If God is willing, but He is not able, He is an impotent, weak God. If He is both able and willing, why doesn't He do something about it?"

Surely this is the quandary that Paul felt two thousand years ago. And it is still the one we feel today.

Elton Trueblood, that rugged Quaker philosopher, put the question most clearly for me years ago. He asked us to suppose what kind of world we would live in if God guaranteed bad things would never happen to Christians.

Suppose that a drunken driver runs a red light and careens into a vehicle being driven by a Christian. As it hits the car, though, that car miraculously sprouts wings and leaps over the drunken driver's car—only because a Christian is inside. Or let's suppose that a jet fan in a Boeing 727 shreds, but because there is a born-again Christian believer on board, the plane miraculously floats to the ground.

Or let's say a fire breaks out in the kitchen of a hotel, but because there is a Christian staying on the tenth floor, the fire miraculously goes out.

You can see how ludicrous the scenarios would be. It would literally mean that we would have a world full of "designated Christians." Think how our society would use such a fact of life. Christians would be put in every car so there would be no accidents, airlines would make sure every flight had at least one Christian aboard and would advertise, "We have a Christian on every flight." And in the big hotel chains, there would be signs that said, "Sleep peacefully with us. There is always a Christian staying in our hotel."

Warren Wiersbe, the great radio preacher, had been speaking somewhat along this vein one Sunday when a man came down to the station and violently criticized him for his belief. "Have you ever read the eleventh chapter of Hebrews, how God delivered all of those heroes of the faith? Abraham, Moses, and all the others who through faith conquered kingdoms, administered justice, gained what was promised, shut the mouths of lions, escaped the edge of the swords. What do you say about them?" he asked Pastor Wiersbe.

Wiersbe, though, knew his Bible a little better than that. He said, "What about verse 35 of Hebrews 11? Look what happened to 'others.' Others were tortured and refused to be released. Some faced years in flogging while others were chained and put in prison. They were stoned and sawed in two, they were put to death by the sword. Faith, my friend, never comes with a guarantee."

A Bonus for Believing?

Faith is its own reward. We cannot expect a rose garden bonus for believing. In reality, we will know many of the same problems as non-Christians and maybe some that non-Christians will never know.

The question is how will we respond. My first reaction to troubles is to be somewhat stoic. Maybe that is what Paul essentially did. You know what I mean—"When the going gets tough, the tough get going" philosophy. Discipline, it says. Brace yourself.

It was a stoic philosophy that caused the captain of the *Titanic* to say as his ship went down, "Be British." And they all knew what he meant. Be tough, keep a stiff upper lip.

But there is a difficulty with such a philosophy. Not everyone has the inner strength of a true stoic. But that's not the real flaw in the idea. The true weakness in being stoic is that stoicism brings glory to the stoic. "Look how tough he is," others will say. "Man, he can hang in there, can't he?"

Dependence on God is not part of the stoic's makeup. At first, anyway. There's always a point where the stoicism runs out— for everyone. And then it can end up in a sort of hypocrisy. The stoic puts on a good face for everyone around him, yet when he or she gets by himself he falls apart.

But Paul never said that stoicism is the answer, even though his writing tells us of his inner toughness. What did he say? In verse 9, the tense of the verb implies that God spoke with finality. It was as if God said, "Now hear this, Paul. Let this ring in your ears from now on." God said, in effect, I want you to understand the sufficiency of My grace: "My grace is sufficient for you . . ."

This is the secret that Christians hold over crises that nonbelievers don't know. Self-sufficient stoicism doesn't last. Crisis coped with alone is crisis that can cripple. God told Paul, in effect, "What is happening to you demonstrates the sufficiency of My grace, and if you learn nothing else you have learned that when you are on your back, the only way you can look is up."

Learn to Lean

First God taught Paul how to lean. And then, second, he told Paul of the perfection of His power. "My power is made perfect in weakness," the Bible says.

Ever notice that when human strength abounds, divine strength is overlooked? When we are strong, when things are going well and we have vast amounts of energy and determination, God's power is almost always overlooked. That's why God told Paul that His power reaches its proper maturity in our weakness.

I believe one of our fundamental mistakes in thinking when

we ponder the reason behind God allowing our suffering is this: we believe God's primary desire is to make us happy.

Well, it's not true. God's primary desire is to make us holy. And sadly, many things that make us happy do not make us holy.

Paul understood that. God's aim was not muddled in Paul's mind. He realized God's aim, and he was able to say, "I will boast all the more gladly about my weaknesses. When I am weak then I am strong."

I haven't reached that point myself. I know very few people who have. But Paul could actually seem to see God's dynamicism hovering over him. Paul had in mind the Shekinah glory, that luminous brightness that hovered over the tabernacle, indicating the presence of God. "The weight of glory hovers over me because of this thorn in my side," Paul seemed to say.

In the words of Dr. J. W. MacGorman, Paul found that the thorn room was the way to the throne room. There was something about the glory of God discovered in suffering that he would have known in no other way.

Dr. Thomas Buford Maston knows what Paul knows. I was his pastor for five years and have been his friend for a dozen. Every clear Sunday, that 88-year-old man and his 87-year-old wife walked the short distance between their church and their home. And as they walked, they pushed a wheelchair in which sat their 60-year-old son, afflicted since birth with cerebral palsy. In those 60 years, there had never been a single night that Dr. Maston was not up six times to help his son.

When Dr. Maston was a Ph.D. student at Yale, he almost died. Through his life, he has had countless troubles. I sat by his hospital bed only a handful of years ago, as he battled for his own life. Out of this latest pain, he wrote his twenty-first book, titled *Walking Like He Walked*. And he would be the first to say that his wisdom is directly related to the power and the presence of God that has come to its right maturity through his own weakness.

Sometimes I wonder about our lopsided look at God's role in blessing and burdens. Think about it. When do we ask, "Why me?" When things are going well? Hardly ever. In fact, insurance companies seem to have the same viewpoint. Their policies chalk up accidents that aren't covered as "acts of God," which has always sounded to me like they're blaming God. I'd love to pick up an insurance policy sometime that had a paragraph in it that said something like "United Mutual Solid Rock Insurance Company wishes to thank God for everything good that happens to this policy holder."

But that's not our mindset. Why do we only ask God, "Why me?" when we are suffering and rarely when we are rejoicing? Paul praised God for his blessings more than he blamed God for his burdens. And therein may be the secret to his understanding and to his positive response to his suffering.

Maybe we shouldn't have the right to ask, "Why me?" when burdens come if we spend a lifetime never thinking "Why me?" when blessings come.

"When I am weak I am strong." Paul found in that truth a dimension that helped him find a way through his pain.

"The presence of God." In that truth, Job found another dimension.

God is working toward making us holy. It is not our understanding we must grapple with, it is our response. Bad things will happen. How we respond will shape how we ultimately will grow.

❧ *11* ❧

Willingness to risk—that's the way the gospel was born.

—— For the kingdom of heaven is as a man travelling into a far country, who called his own servants, and delivered unto them his goods.

And unto one he gave five talents, to another two, and to another one; to every man according to his several ability; and straightway took his journey.

Then he that had received the five talents went and traded with the same, and made them other five talents. And likewise he that had received two, he also gained other two.

But he that had received one went and digged in the earth, and hid his lord's money.

After a long time the lord of those servants cometh, and reckoneth with them.

And so he that had received five talents came and brought other five talents, saying, Lord, thou deliveredst unto me five talents: behold, I have gained beside them five talents more.

His lord said unto him, Well done, thou good and faithful servant: thou hast been faithful over a few things, I will make thee ruler over many things: enter thou into the joy of thy lord.

He also that had received two talents came and said, Lord, thou deliveredst unto me two talents: behold, I have gained two other talents beside them.

His lord said unto him, Well done, good and faithful servant; thou hast been faithful over a few things, I will make thee ruler over many things: enter thou into the joy of thy lord.

Then he which had received the one talent came and said, Lord, I knew thee that thou art an hard man, reaping where thou hast not sown, and gathering where thou hast not strawed:

And I was afraid, and went and hid thy talent in the earth: lo, there thou hast that is thine.

His lord answered and said unto him, Thou wicked and slothful servant, thou knewest that I reap where I sowed not, and gather where I have not strawed:

Thou oughtest therefore to have put my money to the exchangers, and then at my coming I should have received mine own with usury.

Take therefore the talent from him, and give it unto him which hath ten talents.

For unto everyone that hath shall be given, and he shall have abundance: but from him that hath not shall be taken away even that which he hath.

And cast ye the unprofitable servant into the outer darkness: there shall be weeping and gnashing of teeth.

Matthew 25:14–30 KJV

Daring
to Risk

If I were to ask you the point of the parable of the talents, what would you reply? This parable is so familiar, so much a part of our Christian education and heritage, that the question seems silly—and the answer obvious.

But what if I were to tell you the real point of this parable was not that we should use the innate "talents" we've been given? What if I said that Christ had another more important, exciting, life-shaping truth in mind as He told this familiar story?

Well, that is exactly what I think. I believe that this famous parable is really about something quite a bit deeper than an admonition to use our God-given talents. This parable is about *taking risks*. And the question it ultimately raises is the kind meant to shape our idea of following Christ. And that question is this:

How Willing Are We to Take a Risk for the Sake of Christ?

Risking. What is it about the idea of taking risks that excites us at the very same time it strikes fear into our hearts? We seem to be in love with the idea—if somebody else is taking the risk. While only a brave, or crazy, minority are daring enough to take chances, the rest of us watch in awe, shaking our heads and exclaiming, "Boy, look at that!"

Recently, I was reading about Dr. Frank Farley, a psychologist at the University of Wisconsin, who has spent twenty years studying risk-taking personalities. His research has identified what he calls the "T" factor. Those who have this "T" factor are those who are willing to risk, either positively or negatively—that is, willing to risk honestly, for the contribution of humanity or self, or willing to risk dishonestly, to the detriment of society through crime.

It's amazing what people like these will do. In the summer of 1985, 150,000 people risked themselves shooting the rapids down the Colorado River, for instance (*U.S. News and World Report*, Aug. 10, 1986, p. 64). And since 1970, 45,000 people have taken up the hobby of hang-gliding—that's strapping gossamer wings on your back and running off the top of a mountain in hopes the air catches you.

And what about the people who take other kinds of risks? There are supposedly 4,000 new people a day entering the stock market. In places like Denver, Colorado, school teachers have brought in stock brokers during the school's lunch break to give them advice on how to pool their money and buy penny stocks— stocks that may triple in a matter of days or just disappear within that same amount of time (*U.S. News and World Report*, May 25, 1985, p. 61). One Georgia wheat farmer recently put $30,000 into wheat futures and within six months, made $300,000. Of course, that caused a rush of others willing to risk in the future of wheat, too. And then there are the state lotteries, where you can risk a little in the chance to reap a lot. In one recent year the New York State lottery (*Time*, May 28, 1984, p. 42) had a pot of 22.1 million dollars. Even Governor Mario Cuomo waited in line 30 minutes to buy $5.00 worth of chances. Yet, believe it or not, those lottery players are three and a half times more likely to be struck by lightning than they are of winning. Maybe those of us who risk like the adrenalin rush it brings—or maybe it's the feeling of escaping the ordinary we are looking for. Whatever the reason, we like the idea of taking risks . . .

. . . to a certain extent, that is. Most of us are really committed to a lifestyle built on playing it safe. We hedge our bets, cover our tracks, we dig in. From anesthetized surgery to homogenized milk, from the womb to the tomb, most of us work hard at avoiding risk as much as possible. And this is where Jesus' story intersects life for most of today.

Use It or Lose It?

The parable of the talents has been subjected to so much lameness, tameness, and sameness that it's almost become the story of the bland leading the bland. We've watered it down, as if Jesus were only teaching a trite moral like, "God gives you talents. Use your talents or you may lose them."

Now, there is truth in such a moral, of course. But that's certainly not all Jesus had to say in this parable. There's so much more—just as there is in all His parables. Christ's parables are not lame little stories with lame little morals. They are outrageous stories about outrageous characters. Think about them—a man who invites strangers to a feast, a woman who bugs a judge, a man who builds his house on sand. These creations of Jesus do bizarre and eccentric things to wake you and me to the realization that the Christian life is not meant to be predictable or conventional.

So, in the parable of the talents, Jesus Christ is not just talking about what we should do with our talents. He's also challenging us. He's saying, "To follow Me is to be willing to risk—to live a lifetime of risk." And that concept speaks of a life of action, taking chances, adventure, expansion, all for the sake of the Lord Jesus Christ.

Learning to be open to risks, though, may be one of the hardest growing pains we can experience as Christians. But at the same time, such a lesson carries with it the potential of astonishing growth, too. Still, it seems against our nature. Our aversion to anything new, anything risky isn't a new attitude. By the time Matthew had collected this story of Jesus into his book, the history of the church shows that things had begun to settle down. The followers of Jesus had decided they would begin leading a conventional, quiet, predictable sort of life as they waited for Jesus to bring in His kingdom.

Yet this story should have stabbed them into a heightened awareness, a vision of the sort of willingness Christ expects from anyone who follows Him. Looking at the parable of the talents from this perspective sheds a whole new light on every part of the story.

The Real Star

First, the five-talent servant and the two-talent servant in the parable are essentially window dressing. They're stage properties to set off more starkly the real star—the servant who was handed one talent of his lord's money and did nothing with it.

Make no mistake. Even holding one talent was an enormous responsibility. A gold talent in New Testament times was worth about $30,000. The five-talent man, then, had to cart away $150,000, the two-talent man $60,000, and the one-talent man $30,000. What makes these amounts even more incredible is comparing them to the standard of living in that day. The daily pay of the wage earner in Jesus' day was a whopping 15 denarii.

But even though he had less than the others, the focus of the parable is on the one-talent servant who refused to risk what his lord had given him—even though the lord made it quite plain that he was given the money for that expressed purpose.

But the servant could not bring himself to act. He seemed paralyzed, immobilized with fear. Because of the heavy responsibility his lord had given him, he couldn't budge. Like so many of us today, he was the typical spectator, the bench-warmer. He stood on the sidelines, never participating in what his lord was doing.

The Timid Sailor

A famous theologian, Reinhold Neibuhr, tells a parable about this parable. It is the story of a young man who left his home in Kansas to be a sailor on a tall-masted sailing ship. On the third day out to sea, the new sailor was commanded to take the watch in the crow's nest, high up the mast. After climbing about halfway up the mast, though, he stopped. He was frozen to the big mast, not able to finish climbing up, and too proud to slink back down and admit he was afraid of heights in front of the seasoned sailors watching. So he took an option that was no option. He simply clutched at the mast and did nothing with the responsibility that he had been given.

The comparison between the sailor and the one-talent servant is obvious. The servant who was given the stuff of life and told to invest it, to risk it for the sake of his lord, could not bring himself to do anything. He froze. He took an option that was no option. He only clutched the talent, never giving it, or himself, a chance.

If we had never heard the parable of the talents and its applications, we might be tempted to think this servant did something commendable or prudent by not taking any risks. After all, he didn't lose what he had. It was a dangerous world out there, and he had no idea whether the prevailing "market" was going up or down. At least he was honest enough to hand back to his lord the exact amount he was given. We might even have expected the lord would understand, pat him on the head, and say something like, "Well, you did the best you could." With that the master would tell him to trot along.

But not so. Jesus had no sympathy for this character in his story. The servant's lord spoke scathing words of judgment against this man who was prudent—but useless. "You wicked and slothful servant!" he yelled at the servant. Then in verse 30, he tells the others to "cast this unprofitable servant out."

The Servant's Sin

What did this poor servant do that was so bad? The lord said to the servant, "You are evil!" The Greek word used here refers to the devil himself. But the really chilling word in this parable is not "evil." It's the word "useless." It is a word which carries with it the idea that the man had become simply a gap, a blank space on the horizon of life. He was null and void, a *zero*. And all because he was simply unwilling to risk anything for the sake of his lord's kingdom.

So, since he was unwilling to be a "gambler," his lord said, "You've become a zero to me, and I'm going to take your opportunity and give it to someone who is willing."

We can't help having sympathy for this man's plight, though. And we can guess the excuses he used, because we are so much like him. We can almost see him stroke his chin as he looks over at the five-talent servant and thinks, *Sure, he can risk himself. His father is Rabbi So-and-so, head of the synagogue. If I had the connections he had, I could take risks, too. He's got a nice little safety net to catch him.* Or maybe he looks at the two-talent servant and thinks, *Well, if I had his personality and ability, I could risk something too. Why, he's always able to land on his feet.* And so, bitter and cynical, he explains away why others can take risks in the kingdom of the master while he does not.

But the worst aspect of his "spectating" was that it warped his perspective of the master himself. In verse 24, the servant says, "Lord, I know that you are a hard man. You reap where you've not sown, you gather where you've not trod." In Jesus' day, sometimes the seed where a landowner sowed would fall over into the next pasture. Since there weren't any well-marked boundaries or fences set, a really grasping man, at harvest time, would cut a great swath into the field of his neighbor, rationalizing that some of the grain might be his.

The Master's True Nature

But this man's lord was anything but that sort of man. He was a kindly lord who at the end of the day liked to nod at his faithful servants and say, "Well done! You've been faithful." But the one-talent servant could no longer see that side of his master. Since he was not throwing himself into what his master was doing, he became blinded by his spectator's view. And he found himself frozen with fear.

We really aren't much different than the one-talent servant, are we? Many of us have become spectators looking on at what God is doing in the church, in the city, and in the world. Our detached view has blinded us to the true nature of our Lord. He slowly begins to look like a hard taskmaster, rather than a Heavenly Father, because we've become a "watcher," rather than a "doer," in God's program.

The sorriest perspective from which to view anything is that of the passive spectator. How do you know what's really happening if you aren't in the game? A fan is forever on the fringe of the real perspective, ignorant of the inside scoop—no matter how dedicated a cheerleader or critic he is of the players. And having a warped perspective, not truly understanding what you are watching, can affect your actions out of all proportion to reality.

In one of his short stories, Edgar Allen Poe tells of a rural farm family for whom the big event of the year was the arrival of the mail order catalog. Every year they would order one gift for the entire family from its pages. This particular year, they ordered a collapsible telescope, and after several long months, the package finally came. Quickly, they unwrapped it, set it up in front of a window, and trained the lens toward a distant building . . . and what they saw horrified them. Before their telescopic lens was a hideous, grotesque monster. Unanimously, they decided it must be doomsday, so they quickly locked the doors and fastened the windows and pulled down the shades, then huddled together waiting for the end. After a long while, the smallest boy in the family noticed that what they saw through the telescopic lens was not a hideous monster on a distant building at all—it was simply a praying mantis on the screen right outside the window.

Here was reality magnified out of all proportion. They saw, but because they had only a spectator's grasp of what they were viewing, their perspective was warped and they drew the wrong conclusions. Have you noticed yourself griping and grumbling lately about what God is doing in the world or about the state of your Christian life? Could it be that you've become a watcher, a spectator, a bench-warmer rather than someone who is actively, eagerly throwing himself or herself into what God is doing? This parable contains that kind of challenge. It is asking, what is your level of risk? And if we are honest, it forces us to ponder the far-reaching answer.

How willing *are* we to take a risk at some level in our lives? Are we willing to march off the map in terms of our own lives? It doesn't take that much to begin—just the willingness to be open to change, to gamble a little. And maybe in doing so, grow a lot. Risk is deciding to involve ourselves in ways we've never done before, asking what the need is and how we can fill it.

Yet, we hesitate. And maybe for good reason. If we could just understand Jesus' use of this story, especially the harsh treatment of the character, a little better. Not one of us wants to be a zero. And none of us want to misunderstand the reason for the parable. Was the servant treated unfairly? He might not have risked anything, but he didn't lose anything either. To our cautious way of thinking, his punishment doesn't fit the "crime." The man wasn't a thief or adulterer or murderer.

Another Version of the Story

That's probably the sort of reaction that the people who first heard this parable would have had, too. Maybe they had heard a similar parable told by the rabbis of their day in which a certain man went on a long journey and divided his goods among his servants, too. One of the servants put his share of goods in exchange and lost it; the other one held on to his share, doing nothing with it at all. When the lord of the servants returned, he rewarded the one who did nothing with the money, holding onto his share. That servant became head of the household. And the man who risked his share and lost? He was rewarded with *capital punishment!*

Quite a bit of difference from Christ's story, isn't it? To our cautious minds, though, the rabbi's story makes more sense. No wonder, after hearing Jesus' stories, the people exclaimed, "We've never heard stories like this before!" Jesus turned their stories upside down. He made their heroes His villains and their villains His heroes. He replaced all the white hats with black ones, and the black ones with white ones—and the people were thunderstruck.

But what was He really saying to these people—and to us—with such outlandish stories? He was saying, "Look, if you follow Me, yet still believe in safety first, then your values are different from Mine." Jesus' words and actions were meant to shake us up, to shake the world up. Yet we don't hear Jesus' parables describing the kingdom of heaven like that at all. They sound somewhat soothing to our "over-trained" ears. The kingdom of heaven is like . . . what? Like a man who dozed by his fireplace . . . .

No, soothing us wasn't Jesus' intention at all. Instead of peaceful images, He gave us brilliant pictures of risk-takers—of people who weren't afraid to give it everything. He said the kingdom of heaven is like a man who found one pearl of great price and was so captured by the beauty of that pearl, so taken by its value, that he liquidated everything he had. He sold out and risked it all in order that he could own that one pearl. That's not soothing—it's exciting, and very risky. Our Lord said that following Him has far more to do with taking that kind of chance than it does simply believing in safety first at all costs.

Yet our churches, made up of believers like you and me, seem to be the least-likely candidates for taking any risk at all. When asked to point out people and organizations that are risk-takers, we point excitedly at the entrepreneur building a big development, or we point to the investor who risks financially on something of value. How often do we point to the church and say, "Look at those people! Look at what they're risking for the sake of Christ!" We as the church are probably the very last ones in the community to risk anything at all. We become too comfortable, too settled to consider change—and in so being, risk becoming zeros, useless bench-warmers, grumbling and mumbling so much that we ultimately miss the action.

"Our Lady of Risk"

In his little book on the parables, George Buttrick tells of visiting an ancient abbey on the coast of France named "Our Lady of the Risk." Unable to figure out why medieval Catholics would name a religious residence hall something like that, he asked the people why. They told him the name "Our Lady of the Risk" was given to the abbey to commemorate the fact that the mother of our Lord Jesus Christ, in reality, took the ultimate risk for a young woman of her age. She was willing to accept the idea, brought by an angel, that she would conceive and give birth to the Messiah—without help from a husband.

We forget today how truly ultimate that risk was for that young woman. In first-century Jewish society, a teenage girl, with child and without husband, took more than the risk of being ostracized. She also risked being stoned.

Yet the gospel began, humanly speaking, when that quiet, godly Jewish girl was willing to look at that angel and say, "Yes. So be it unto me, according to your word. I'm willing to take the risk, for the sake of the kingdom of God." Willingness to risk—that's the way the gospel was born.

When we compare Mary's story and the risk she was willing to take with Christianity today, our lifestyle does look awfully lame and same and tame. How conventional, predictable, our Christian living has become. But, what should such a comparison mean for us individually? *Are the spotlights on me?* we may begin to wonder. "Does Christ expect *me*—normal, average *me*—to risk something for him?" we ask.

The answer is yes. Of all people, Christ knew what risk was—and He knew the magnitude of being willing to risk. When He died on the cross, in a very real way, He took the ultimate risk. He hung there from about 9 in the morning to 3 in the afternoon only because He believed, with His whole being, that God would keep faith with Him and raise Him on the third day. How did He know? Did He have a guarantee? A signed, notarized piece of paper saying, "Yes, My Son, I agree to raise You on the third day"? He had nothing—nothing but the willingness to risk and the only guarantee we all have, the word of the Father that if we risk for Him, He will honor it. But that was enough for Christ. With that assurance alone, He took the chance of the cross by saying, "I'm willing to risk the cost for the sake of the world, because I believe in the word of the Father."

Where Do We Fit In?

What can we do? How can we change? There's a place where we can move away from the commonness, and risk the unusual for Christ. Somewhere in our routine, somewhere in our daily lives is the place where God wants us to make a detour. It could be a road He wants us to cross, an encounter He wants us to have, a confrontation He wants us to face, a word He wants us to speak, a deed He wants us to do. To us, it looks like a risk. Our first response is, "I've never done that before . . ." But that may be the very place where Christ wants us to step out in faith and risk that something different for Him.

I'm willing, but . . . what if I fail? we think. The parable of the talents closes with an answer. It deals with the importance of taking responsibility instead of passing the buck. In verse 19, we see a biblical image of judgment when the lord returns and beckons his servants to him. The Lord Jesus Christ is coming back, it seems to say, just as the lord in this parable came back after a long time away. And what is the first thing the lord in the parable does? He made his servants answer one question: Had they been willing to risk for the sake of his kingdom while he was gone?

"Well done!" the master said to the five-talent servant and the two-talent servant. And then he rewarded them even more. And then the focus changes to the one-talent man who played it safe. And what is the servant's first response? One we all know intimately. He immediately began to make excuses. His first excuse was fear. He said, "I was afraid, so I went and hid it."

Of what was he really afraid? We know he was afraid of the tough image he had conjured up for his lord. But could there have been something else? Could he have been afraid that if he had given his best, it wouldn't have been as good as the five-talent servant's or the two-talent man's? After all, *he* only had one talent. Very easily, his fear may have been that instead of going off like a Roman candle and lighting up the whole sky for his lord, he might have fizzled out.

We can all identify with that fear. Actually, more than anything else, this fear may be what keeps *us* from risking. It's not that we don't want to give our best. We're worried that our best won't be good enough.

But Christ didn't tell us that we have to succeed. He *did* tell us that we need to risk in whatever way He asks, at whatever level He asks. So many of us are willing, but we just don't think what we could do will be as good as what others will do. So what happens? Nothing. Nothing at all. For fear of not doing the best, we freeze and simply do nothing. We're immobilized with the fear that our best won't be good enough, and that God will agree.

A Self-fulfilling Prophecy

When the one-talent man said, "I knew that you were a hard man," he had visualized himself as a victim. And that's always a self-fulfilling prophecy. He said, "I knew this wouldn't work out. I knew I couldn't please you, so I didn't do anything." But while he was mumbling, he missed two very important truths about his lord and about those who risk.

First, all of those willing to risk for the sake of Christ belong to the same order of heroes. That's worthy of repeating: *All who are willing to risk for the sake of Christ belong to the same order of heroes.* God knows our capacity to risk, and He knows our capacities vary. That's why He gave varied abilities, some five talents, some two, and some one. But notice that the words to the five-talent servant are exactly the same words the lord used to praise the two-talent servant. "Well done, good and faithful servant," he said to both. "Welcome, I'm going to give you more."

The Point of the Parable

And that's the ultimate point of the parable. To risk *to your potential* makes us heroes in the sight of our Lord. How is that possible? It's because God has already tilted the game of life in favor of those who risk for Him. We don't live in a universe that's controlled by an impersonal computer. We live in a universe where the game has already been tilted by a nail-scarred hand. If we're willing to risk our potential, we'll find we won't always win, but in the end, we'll find it all to be tilted our way.

And how do we find our potential? Everyone has a different threshold of risk. And it is that threshold the Lord wants us to cross. He is the Lord of risk. So the goal is to discover what our threshold is. What line do I have to cross which takes all my spiritual stamina? It could be just crossing the street, or crossing the hall, or it could be crossing the world—using our five talents, our two talents, or our one. But the only way to find out is to gamble, to risk that first step. To take the dare. "If you seek to save your life, you'll lose it," the Lord of risk said. "If you lose it for My sake, you'll find it." The life of the Christian shouldn't be boring or predictable. It should be an ever-changing panorama of challenge and excitement.

The parable of the talents shows us how—and more importantly—why.

❧ *12* ❧

When we make a move toward God, He is making a move toward us.
And . . . . will abundantly restore us.

Return, O Israel, to the Lord your God.
   Your sins have been your downfall!
Take words with you
   and return to the Lord.
Say to him:
   "Forgive all our sins
and receive us graciously,
   that we may offer the fruit of our lips.
Assyria cannot save us;
   we will not mount war-horses.
We will never again say 'Our gods'
   to what our own hands have made,
      for in you the fatherless find compassion."

"I will heal their waywardness
   and love them freely,
      for my anger has turned away from them.
I will be like the dew to Israel;
   he will blossom like a lily.
Like a cedar of Lebanon
   he will send down his roots;
      his young shoots will grow.
His splendor will be like an olive tree,
   his fragrance like a cedar of Lebanon.
Men will dwell again in his shade.
   He will flourish like the grain.
He will blossom like a vine,
   and his fame will be like the wine from Lebanon.
O Ephraim, what more have I to do with idols?
   I will answer him and care for him.
I am like a green pine tree;
   your fruitfulness comes from me."

Who is wise? He will realize these things.
   Who is discerning? He will understand them.
The ways of the Lord are right;
   the righteous walk in them,
      but the rebellious stumble in them.

Direction —
Getting Back to God

During the Korean War some ten million families were divided and displaced. Families were torn apart. In 1983, thirty years later, the Korean Broadcasting System tried something extraordinary to reunite them. A long telethon was aired that showed at fifteen-second increments those who had been separated from loved ones. Each segment showed the faces of these people holding a plaque that listed their names, the circumstances under which they disappeared, and where they might be contacted.

It was a national phenomenon. Immediately, 3,000 people were restored to relationships that had been dead. And it all happened right on the television screen—reunions filled with screams and shouts and sighs and tears. Even the host of the program couldn't keep from crying. The telethon was watched by 78 percent of the viewing audience of the entire nation. The demand was so great that the telethon was continued for several more days and now, several years later, this telethon of reconciliation is still being run every Friday night.

There is something in the human heart that loves to see

people coming home, getting back together. Think back to the last time the nightly news told of a long-lost sister or mother or son being found. How often we've seen television films of such reunions at some airport's terminal gate. Maybe that is why there is a timeless appeal about the story of Hosea, a man who lived over 2800 years ago.

Hosea was a simple Hebrew man who loved his wife Gomer. Yet one day she left him to become a prostitute. Hosea would not accept that decision on her part and vowed to use every means in his power to get her back. Sure enough, one day he saw her for sale at a slave market and bought her back. Gomer, though she was soiled merchandise, was gladly, freely taken back by Hosea as his loved and cherished wife.

The analogy between Hosea and God may be obvious. It is assuredly the reason this story is in the Bible. But the analogy is a wonderful one. In essence, God is more like Hosea in his quest for reconciliation than Hosea was. There is no length to which God will not go to see that we are back with Him. Our God, our loving God, receives us just as unconditionally, on just as simple terms as Hosea did with Gomer.

There are times in life when we find ourselves separated— away—from our Lord. We somehow lose direction, look away for a moment that turns into days, then weeks and months. For some, it is even years. On the day that we wake up to our separation from Him, we experience the sinking feeling that maybe we are too far away to ever come back.

There is a time for coming back, though. And God is a Hosea pursuing us, even when we act as if we want nothing to do with Him. It's difficult for us to believe that when we've strayed so far. But it's true. The Book of Hosea convinces us of this truth in several ways.

Return

God actively longs for us to return. The very first word of this chapter of Hosea is "Return, O Israel, to the Lord your God.

Take words with you and return to the Lord." Fifteen times in the Book of Hosea the word "return" is used. In Hosea's language it is a word that came to mean to backtrack to where you left God until you are back where you belong.

Jeremiah uses the word "return" a hundred times in his prophecy. The Book of Hosea continues the same loving appeal. The door is open from God's side—if we'll come back He'll receive us. It is a book about love that simply wants a chance. Hosea kept telling Gomer that if she would give his love a chance he'd show her that she could come back. He kept telling Gomer, "The door is open." And as Hosea told his story, he came to realize that God is like that, too.

This isn't a warning to those who are about to slip. This is for those who have already slipped. Hosea's original audience was the Old Testament Israel that had already faced disaster and calamity. The nation was ruined. At this time, the final invasion of Shalmaneser V, the awful conqueror had ruined Northern Israel. Hosea believed God to be saying: "Israel, even though you are already broken and ruined, if you will come back to Me I promise we can start over again together."

Why is it that we hesitate at such an invitation? We are living in such pain and missing the growth such a spiritual reconciliation offers. We know we can come back. Yet we hesitate. Isn't it because every mile we go down the track away from God makes it harder to come back—because we fear that reunion?

It must have been like that for Gomer when she sold herself the first time. It must have been hard. But the second and third time it became easier. The farther she got away from Hosea the easier the separation became—and the more impossible the return seemed. She was too aware of how she had flagrantly abused his love—and she couldn't bear the thought of seeing him face to face.

Several years ago, a sixteen-year-old Florida girl was dropped off at school by her mother. As she was getting out of the car, she waved to her mother and said, "I'll see you tonight." But her mother did not see her again for two and a half years. The girl disappeared. The girl's parents exhausted their bank account, borrowed money from friends, and took off from their jobs to instigate a nationwide search for their daughter. Finally, someone saw the girl's picture down in Georgia, called her parents, and they drove to Georgia and found her.

Do you know what her story was? She said, "I was just tired of school and I met some friendly strangers and they took me to a bus stop. I had enough money to get to Georgia, and every mile down the road I grew more fearful of coming back and facing you. And every mile further away, the easier it was to go another mile. You remember all those telephone calls that hung up before you answered? That was me." They found hundreds of letters she had written to her parents but never mailed. She didn't know that while she was running from them, they were running toward her in love.

That's the story of Hosea. Even though we may be running as this sixteen-year-old was, fearing the reunion, the moment of truth when we face God again, Hosea's story is in the Bible to tell us it is a reunion we do not have to fear. The Florida girl said if she had known that her parents loved her so much, she would have come back on her own. That may have been exactly what Gomer said, too. It is certainly what we can say.

But how do we go about coming back? What do we say? How is it done? Hosea tells us how. He says, "Take words with you and return to the Lord." Hosea's audience had drifted so far away from God that they didn't even know what to tell Him, so Hosea is saying, in essence, "Here's what to say to God. Repeat after me: 'Forgive us our sins and receive us graciously.'"

Ritual Replaces Reality

To find our direction back again, our first step is to have a real, live conversation with God. We should talk to Him.

The Book of Hosea is the story of a people who had once belonged to God but allowed rituals to displace reality. They let the mechanics of a dead religion replace the meaning of a living faith. They lost direction because they mixed religion up with God. Earlier in his story Hosea stated that when these people would go with their flocks and their herds to seek the Lord, they would not find Him because He had withdrawn Himself from them. Christ quoted Hosea 6:6 to the religious leaders of His day, telling them to go find out what it meant: "I desire mercy, not sacrifice, and the acknowledgment of God rather than burnt offerings."

Hosea's generation was doing everything right, according to their religion's rituals . . . they were bringing their animal sacrifices, they were mumbling the right chants, whispering the right songs—but they were not having personal communion with God.

It's easy to see how ritual replaces reality, even in little things. The custom of shaking hands, a common action we take every day, began back in ancient Babylon. The king at his coronation would go up to the statue of the pagan god and shake his stone hand. Supposedly this was a transfer of power to the king. Then, in the Middle Ages, knights shook hands to show that they weren't bearing a weapon. Now, it has become a ritual without any reality to it.

Ever wonder why visiting dignitaries are given the "key" to a city by its mayor? That ritual goes all the way back to the Middle Ages, too, when there were walls around every city, and the city gates were locked. Now it is another empty ritual with no reality about it at all. It's just a gesture, a courtesy.

Little by little, if we are not careful, we can become just like ancient Israel in our religious life. We lose direction without noticing it; we drift away into aimless ritual. It can happen to anyone. This mindless emotional and spiritual wandering can separate us from God as certainly as some heinous sin. And possibly, there are many more of us who lose our direction through routine religiosity, going further and further away like the Florida girl, than there are those who lose our way through outright immorality. Hosea is saying, "Talk to God. Don't lose reality in your ritual."

Renunciation

But then Hosea mentions the other aspect of coming back to God. He says, when we come back, we must be willing to make a "renunciation." Hosea again gave them the words: "Azariah cannot save us, we will not mount war-horses, we will never again say 'Our gods' to what our hands have made." He states that they must make two vows of renunciation concerning dependence on other things. And so, of course, should we.

1) We must renounce ultimate dependence on everything outside of ourselves, beyond God. What does the phrase, "Azariah cannot save us," mean? At the time of Hosea Israel had become obsessed with the power of its Northern neighbors. Those neighbors were smart. They had mathematics, a thriving economy, and a strong military force. Every time Israel was caught in a corner, instead of putting their dependence on the living God, they would run to this pagan nation for help.

But before we shake our heads at those fickle Israelites, maybe we should try filling in the sentence ourselves:

_____ cannot save me.

What did you put in the blank? We can probably name several things we've looked to for help, placing our ultimate trust and dependence upon. Maybe it is a parent. Every time things go bad we go to Mom or Dad. Maybe it's a habit. When life gets tough, we reach for the bottle. Maybe it's work that we plunge ourselves into. God wants us to make that statement, to say and believe that no relationship outside the one we have with Him deserves our ultimate dependence.

2) Next, we are to renounce ultimate dependence on every internal resource except God. Hosea says, "We will not mount war-horses." We are not to trust ultimately in ourselves, in our own resources alone, either. Of course, this goes against the "rugged individual" concept that we Americans love so much. We lean more toward admiring the one who says, "When the going gets tough, I'm one of the toughs who gets going." But we may also depend on our talents or our connections or our charms. We believe these things are forever, to be relied upon, but we have no

guarantees that any of this—our health, our talents, our fortitude—will be enough to get us through life. When we come back to God, we need to come in absolute dependence upon Him. And when we do, we'll be surprised how quickly God will run to meet us. It's as James 4:8 tells us: "If we draw near to God, God is already drawing near to us."

A pastor friend of mine once told a story about a time when he was involved in building a new educational wing in his church. He told of walking through the building, just to bask in a sense of accomplishment and pride. No one was around. The staff had gone, the construction crew was gone, and it was getting dark. He tiptoed over the debris and noticed a room he'd never entered. So he walked in and let go of the door—and then he realized that there was no doorknob on the inside of the door.

Although it was dark inside, he didn't panic. He just waited for his eyes to adjust. And that's when he saw the other man in the room with him. The pastor could barely see him. So he said, "Can I help you?" which translates into, "What are you doing here?" But the man didn't answer. That's when the pastor began to notice that the man was bigger than he was and that he looked very ugly. So the pastor prayed, "Lord, I need more light, lots more light." And then he turned straight toward the man and said, "What are you doing in this room?!" The man still did not reply. The pastor thought he was in serious trouble, so he reached back for the door and when he did, he saw that he wasn't in the room with another man, he was in a room with a mirror.

We're just like that in our relationship with God at one time or another, aren't we? It seems dark, and we make a move and then worry about the moves that others will make back. And yet most of our fears are caused by our own reflection. When we make a move toward God, He is making a move toward us. And if we do that, God will abundantly restore us.

Restoration

How will God act? He restores us graciously. As Hosea puts it, God says, "I will heal their waywardness or this apostasy." For centuries, the Israelites had bungled their relationship with God.

God offered not to treat the symptoms if they started that dialogue again with Him, but to touch their lives in such a way as to get rid of that wayward inclination.

Many of us have trouble with committing the same failure over and over. We figure there is no way He will take us back over and over again. But God is saying here that He can get rid of that inclination toward waywardness. He can help us start again.

The illustrations Hosea used to explain God's characteristics involved with this restoration are beautiful. First He will restore us to wholeness by giving us life where there was no life. According to Hosea, God says, "I will be like the dew to Israel." In that arid climate, dew was as essential as it was mysterious and trustworthy. Through the heat of the summer, the only thing that kept the plants alive was the dew. As little as three-hundredths of an inch of dew collects on the leaves of the plants and yet that alone mysteriously gives them life. And it shows up every morning, giving life in a mysterious and trustworthy way.

Second, God will help us blossom like a lily. The flower that Hosea had in mind was a flower that grew in the desert among the cracks and rocks and thorn bushes. These flowers are beauty in the midst of ugliness in the midst of unlikeliness. God's promise is that He can bring beauty out of our ugliness. No matter how unlikely our situation, we can blossom.

And third, God will give us stability where there has only been instability. The figure of speech used here is the cedar of Lebanon. The root system of this cedar is at least as expansive and extensive as its system of shoots above ground. In that arid country the cedar must put down an amazing amount of roots to find life-sustaining moisture. The result is a tree that is sturdy, stable, unwavering. Wouldn't we all like to be that stable? But that stability is another promise involved with God's response to our return.

And then in a wonderful summary image, God is pictured as an evergreen tree. "I am a God for all seasons," the image seems to be saying. "I am a God for all the seasons of your life. In every area of your life from this moment on, I will be your great resource." Hosea was Gomer's great resource. He brought her back, loved her, and grew old with her. He was with her through every season of the rest of her life.

And God is like that. He is searching for us, offering reconciliation, regardless of how far away we've wandered, regardless of why we've wandered, always giving us hope for tomorrow. And this hope extends not only to the end of our earthly lives—but into the endless life beyond. The *Growing Pains of the Soul* prepare that soul for eternity!

Study Guide

1. *Defeating Depression*

1. How do you react to the statement, "Christians should not become depressed"?
2. Does the fact that the prophet Jeremiah suffered from depression help or hinder you in terms of your own spiritual life?
3. Have you ever "scolded" God when being honest in prayer?
4. What forms of rejection do you feel you have experienced?
5. What two lessons does the author emphasize on p. 24?
6. What is the third lesson on p. 26?

2. *Winning over Worry*

1. Analyze the author's claim that one-seventh of the Sermon on the Mount is devoted to worry. Do you agree?
2. React to the three questions asked at the bottom of p. 33.
3. Define "Lordly logic" in your own words.
4. What two illustrations of "worry-free living" does Jesus list?

3. *Grappling with Guilt*

1. Contrast "real" and "false" guilt.
2. What other biblical examples of guilt can you name?
3. What three dimensions of guilt does the author list?
4. Discuss the author's statement, "If you don't deal with your guilt, it *will* deal with you."
5. What does it mean to you that Christ is your "Advocate"?

4. *Security—Will God Protect Me?*

1. What experience or event has caused you the greatest fear?
2. How did you react to the author's "eagle" story on pp. 59–60?
3. Have you ever experienced what you felt was angelic protection?

4. What do you think motivated General MacArthur's bravery in the story on p. 65?
5. Where does your security lie?

5. Testing—Handling Life's Tough Times

1. What are the four typical reactions to testing given on p. 69?
2. What is the Christian's reaction to be?
3. Describe in your own words "the joy of the Lord."
4. What two characteristics of our faith are strengthened by testing (p. 76)?

6. Hidden Weakness—The Sinkhole Syndrome

1. Trace the steps by which King Saul changed from a humble and obedient servant-leader to an arrogant and disobedient misfit.
2. Why is it that we sometimes fail where we should be strongest?
3. Look at some of the moral failures in the news today (both Christian and political). Do you think our world is more corrupt today than it was in Saul's time? In Jesus' time?
4. Compare the words of Saul at the beginning and end of his career.

7. Releasing the Past—Holy Amnesia

1. What event or experience from your past causes you to feel guilt?
2. What event or experience from your past causes you to feel pride?
3. Do either of these memories hinder your spiritual walk?
4. What happens when we concentrate on a spiritual goal?
5. How is spiritual goal-setting similar to athletic goal-setting?

8. When Faith Causes Problems

1. Have you ever experienced problems because of your faith?
2. How do you react to the author's statement, ". . . when our faithfulness causes problems, God's faithfulness will see us through" (p. 103)?
3. Do you agree with the author's appraisal of typical newsmagazines and their attitude toward evangelicals? Are any fair in their appraisal?
4. Have you ever felt rejected as Moses did? What happened to change things?
5. Discuss D. L. Moody's evaluation of Moses' life given on pp. 108–109. Can you think of others about whom this might be said?
6. "Our faith stands on knowing that God does what He says He will do in His name" (p. 110). Discuss.

9. Forgiveness—Disgracing Grace

1. Try to answer the question on p. 115: "How can anyone who has been wronged by another human being possibly be so forgiving as to *keep* on forgiving?"

2. Of our talents, the author says, "Time, money, energy, connections, influence, contacts, life itself—all are gifts" (p. 117). Discuss the ramifications of this as it relates to the way we live our lives.
3. Have you ever felt relief and thanksgiving similar to what Dr. Gregory describes on p. 118? Think about it—or talk about it.
4. Discuss Luther's statement: "When you have experienced Christ, you must go out to be like Christ toward others" (p. 120).
5. What are the three steps in the process of forgiveness?

10. Crisis—Why Me?

1. Discuss the "four friends" who visited the woman in the hospital.
2. Do you have any "thorns"—or do any of your loved ones?
3. Have you ever asked "why?"
4. How did Job respond to the suffering he endured?
5. What do you think of the author's hypothetical illustrations on pp. 132–133?
6. "Faith is its own reward" (p. 133). Do you agree? What does this mean?
7. We often ask, "Why me?" Is it better to ask, "Why not me?"

11. Daring to Risk

1. What lessons does Dr. Gregory see in the parable of the talents?
2. Do you agree that Jesus is saying in effect, "To follow Me is to be willing to risk? To live a lifetime of risk"? Does this concept excite or scare you?
3. How do you feel about the "use it or lose it" idea? Discuss.
4. Which would you rather be—a participant or a spectator?
5. What kind of people do you feel most comfortable with—risk-takers or those who play it safe?
6. Who is "Our Lady of Risk"?
7. Which of the servants do you most easily identify with?

12. Direction—Getting Back to God

1. Have you ever felt like running away—from a person or a situation?
2. Have you ever run away from a life situation you could not handle?
3. Hosea talks about "return" and "renunciation." What is involved when a wanderer returns? What do we need to renounce?
4. What are the four aspects of our "restoration" by God?